PILLAGED!

How they are looting £413 million a
day from your savings and pensions

... and what to do about it

David Craig

GIBSON SQUARE

My thanks to Aviva, Legal & General and NPI, whose brilliance in taking my money convinced me of the need to write this book

First published in the UK in 2011 by

Gibson Square

Tel: +44 (0)20 7689 4790

info@gibsonsquare.com
www.gibsonsquare.com

Contents

Why worry?

- Every year about £105 billion (£105,000,000,000) — £413 million each working day — is siphoned off from our savings and pensions by people in the financial services industry.

- Over the thirty years that most of us save — from the ages of about thirty five to sixty five — we'll see over three trillion pounds looted from our money.

- This is making financial services insiders rich beyond our wildest dreams.

- Yet most of us get negligible interest on our savings, our pension funds hardly grow and any investments in unit trusts and shares usually fail to match the mouthwatering returns regularly trumpeted in the weekend newspaper ads

- Almost all the growth in our savings, investments and pensions is taken by fund managers, salespeople and financial advisers.

- Some of us may even end up paying a third to a half of our savings to the people who manage our money.

- Seven out of ten of us will not have enough money to retire in comfort.

- Unless we understand how our money is being taken and how to protect our savings, our money will continue to pour through our hands into other people's pockets.

- Remember: your money may just be someone else's end-of-year bonus.

The need for this book

Each year in Britain, over £105 billion (£105,000,000,000) of our money is taken from us and put in the pockets of the people who manage our savings, pensions and investments. That's about £413 million every single working day. Most of us will probably save for about thirty years – say from the age of thirty five till we retire in our mid to late sixties. During these thirty or so years, what we could call our 'savings life', over three trillion pounds – £3,150,000,000,000 – will be effortlessly sliced from our money by the people who handle it for us. This is an almost unimaginable amount of money.

If our savings were regularly increasing in value and if most of us could look forward to a reasonably comfortable retirement, then handing over £413 million a day to financial services insiders to look after our money might be justifiable. But many ordinary people have seen the returns on their savings collapse, their pension funds struggle to produce enough money for them to consider retirement at all and their investments fail to achieve anything like the mouth-watering growth seemingly promised in the unit trust ads in the weekend newspapers.

With governments in most Western countries horrifically in debt, with job security disappearing and with all but a handful of companies getting rid of final-salary pensions, we can no longer rely on the state or our employers to provide for our financial futures. Increasingly we have to take responsibility for our own finances. Yet, as we are encouraged to pour ever more of our money into banks, building societies, pension funds, shares and unit trusts, it is far from obvious that we are being well served for the £413 million a day taken from us by the financial services industry. In fact, it often seems as if whatever happens with interest rates, stock markets and the economy, the only winners are those who are fortunate enough to get their hands on our savings while we ordinary savers are being taken for mugs.

We cannot allow this to continue. We have to get more for our money if we are ever to build any kind of financial security for ourselves and our families. That's why I've written *Pillaged*. I want to warn people about the huge number of varied, ingenious and sometimes deceitful ways financial professionals are siphoning off our money making themselves £413 million a day richer and us £413 million a day poorer in the process. Only by understanding what is going on can we ever hope to fight back against those who so eagerly take our money and only by knowing the many tricks and traps which make us poorer can we ever have a chance of securing our own financial futures.

Introduction

Losing my financial virginity

Entering the financial jungle

In late March 2010, I was in my local bank paying in a couple of cheques. Noticing that I had a few thousand pounds in my current account as a result of some work I had been doing, the cashier suggested I could get better returns if I invested the money, rather than have it languishing where it was earning almost no interest. Helpfully, the cashier said she would arrange a meeting for me with the bank's financial adviser who could give me some ideas about how to get more from my money. As the meeting was free, I agreed.

About a week later I went for my appointment. While waiting to see the adviser, I overheard two of the bank's investment people joking about what they were going to say to a pensioner who had just found out that he had lost almost half his life savings by putting them in a supposedly 'cautious' investment sold to him by the bank. Slightly perturbed, I was ushered into the bank manager's cavernous office where the financial adviser was waiting to help me.

After a bit of introductory chit chat, I revealed that I knew next to nothing about savings, investments and pensions as I'd been busy working for the last twenty or so years and had never had time to try to understand how to get the best from my money. I also admitted that I had most of my hard-earned cash sitting in various longer-term, previously high-interest bank and building society accounts. Seeing he was dealing with someone who was a financial ignoramus and who had years of savings potentially available to be invested, I suddenly seemed to become the financial adviser's best friend – and he apparently mine. Getting out some brochures, he enthusiastically told me I was really lucky as, just the week before, my bank had launched an exciting new product – a stock-market bond which would give me a hundred and twenty per cent of any growth in the stock-market index over five years. But if the index fell, the bank generously guaranteed it would return my original investment in full. So whatever happened, I apparently couldn't lose. The adviser stressed that this investment would only be available for a limited time, so it would be best if I acted quickly. It all seemed pretty convincing. But being a monumental coward and an irrepressible cynic, I said I would think over the financial adviser's proposal and made my escape.

Shortly after my meeting at the bank, I received statements from a couple of pension schemes to which I was contributing. When I started the pension plans the salesmen had assured me that my savings would grow by anything from five to nine per cent a year tax-free and could be worth hundreds of thousands of pounds by the time I retired. But looking at the results, I was disappointed to notice that my pension pot had not grown at all - for quite a few years. In fact, my savings had regularly shrunk thanks to the poor performance of the funds and the generous fees the pension companies had been extracting for themselves from me year after year.

All this set me wondering if I and the unfortunate pensioner were the only people being sold financial products whose value we couldn't judge and pension savings plans which seemed to shrivel rather depressingly in the harsh, cold light of economic reality. Having spent most of my working life as a management consultant analysing the performance of over a hundred organisations around the world, I decided to use some of the consulting tricks I had learnt to investigate how the financial services industry operated and to find out what we ordinary savers got, or more often didn't get, for our money. First I did a quick number crunch and almost fell off my chair when I found that the financial services industry was siphoning off around £413 million every working day – £105 billion a year – from its customers' savings and pensions. This intrigued me – how could these people fleece their customers of so much money without many people realising what was happening? Over the following couple of months I read a small mountain of books about investing; held meetings with financial advisers from several banks; met with independent financial advisers and pension planners; bought a rather expensive subscription to a money management magazine; signed up for loads of electronic investment newsletters; and attended presentations by wealth managers, seminars by investment specialists and webinars by all kinds of other self-proclaimed finance industry experts, all promising to reveal the secrets of how I could make my money grow, become wealthy and live a life of ease free from financial worries.

Unfortunately, I never did discover how to get rich. This could have been because I was too stupid to understand the pearls of financial wisdom being so liberally cast my way. But more probably it was because I had naively stumbled into a jungle crowded with unusually hungry people who were mainly interested in relieving me of as much of my money as they thought they could legally get away with. After a couple of months discovering the many ways that financial industry insiders could make themselves wealthy at my expense, I thought it worth writing *Pillaged* to warn others about the dangers facing all of us as we try to make our way through the financial jungle that we will all have to cross during our lives.

Frankenstein takes control

The financial services industry used to be mainly concerned with looking after people's savings and lending money to homebuyers and businesses. But that was a long time ago. Today, financial services have become a massive, obscenely profitable money-making machine. In Britain, three of our biggest banks have grown so large that each of them has potential liabilities that are equal to what the whole country earns in a year. With huge size has come huge power. In spite of the platitudes of our posturing politicians and the feeble efforts of our useless regulators, the major financial institutions do what they want. Government ministers may implore the main banks to show some restraint with their salaries and restrict their bonuses, but the banks contemptuously ignore them. And although the main regulator, the Financial Services Authority (FSA) has seen its budget grow from around £20 million to nearer £400 million since Gordon Brown expanded its powers in 1997 and although its bosses have paid themselves record performance bonuses over the last few years, the FSA's performance has been worse than dismal – it didn't notice that several of the major banks it was meant to be monitoring were bankrupt and has repeatedly failed to protect ordinary savers against outlandish profiteering and recidivist mis-selling by many of our best known and most respected financial institutions.

The secret of our disappearing savings

This has left us largely at the mercy of a finance industry that slices off a surprisingly impressive chunk of all the money we manage to save and invest. With many financial products, we've no idea how much we are paying in fees, commissions, management charges, dealing costs and all kinds of other expenses. When the management charges are disclosed, we will usually be told that they are around one to two per cent a year. But too often this is just a small part of the story and the real level of deductions will be at least two to three times the published figure.

Still, two or three or even four per cent may seem like pretty small numbers to many people. But over time these charges can easily cut a third or more off the money we hope to accumulate. So, for example, if we wanted an extremely modest inflation-protected income of say £3,500 a year in addition to our state pension, we'd have generate around £150,000 in savings, pensions, unit trusts and other bits and pieces during our working life - £100,000 to provide our £3,500 a year income and another £50,000 to give to the people handling our money. If we wanted slightly more substantial inflation-protected earnings of around £15,000 a year in addition to the state pension, we'd have to generate wealth of a massive £600,000 or thereabouts – we'd need around £400,000 to fund our £15,000 a year income and about £200,000 to pay financial services insiders' fees, management charges, commissions and various other expenses. And this is just for putting our savings into simple mainstream financial products. If we have bought some of the more complex and expensive products like with-profits schemes or stock-market bonds, all eagerly pushed on us by banks, journalists and financial advisers or if we've been a victim of mis-selling, we could easily see up to half of our money mysteriously disappearing from our savings and then miraculously reappearing in someone else's bank account.

How investing can be bad for our wealth

Bringing up a family and having a reasonable standard of living while also saving a few hundred thousand pounds may feel like quite a challenge. But, if we also want a decent lifestyle in retirement with a few Caribbean cruises and other holidays in the sun, we're going to need considerably more than that. To get an inflation-protected income in retirement of say £30,000 a year, unless we are an MP, work for the public sector or are part of a final-salary pension scheme, we're going to have to build up close to £1 million in assets in addition to our homes. Either willingly or reluctantly, most of us will have to become fairly diligent savers and investors.

Putting several hundred thousand pounds aside could be quite hard work for a lot of us. Some of us may be happy to take a gamble with our money and buy shares, bonds, unit trusts, gold, rare stamps, agricultural land, moringa plantations or other hopefully lucrative investments. But even if we're allergic to risking our money ourselves, the companies managing our pensions will be throwing hundreds of billions, including our pension savings, into all sorts of things ranging from relatively safe government bonds to highly speculative hedge funds and complex new financial instruments that they probably don't understand.

Financial industry firms will try to attract our money by telling us about the great returns we'll make – unit trust salespeople, bank advisers, pension planners and various others will enthusiastically do projections for us showing how our wealth will grow at seven, nine or even more per cent a year, magically seeming to turn modest sums into hundreds of thousands of pounds over twenty or thirty years. They'll be supported by ever-acquiescent personal finance journalists eager to puff the products of whatever company is putting most advertising their employer's way. One excited journalist recently wrote an article praising the benefits of stock markets by demonstrating how just £1,000 invested in shares in 1926 would be worth over £72 million today. All this sales talk sounds great, but unfortunately the reality for most of us is usually quite different.

Of course, we can theoretically make money from investing. Some people do. But the disappointing truth is that over the longer term, shares give annual growth of just five to six per cent a year after inflation and pension funds only around four per cent. This poses a not inconsequential problem for us ordinary savers – if we're paying three per cent a year or more in all kinds of charges, commissions and fees while our investments are only growing by four to six per cent a year, it's actually going to take between five hundred and a thousand years to transform £1,000 into £72 million rather than just eighty four years as the journalist claimed.

Luckily we don't all need £72 million. Supposing we manage to find ways of reducing the fees and charges we pay and getting slightly better returns than the average saver, then perhaps a few per cent a year growth after paying charges may not be too bad. Unfortunately there's a catch. While shares and pensions on average may provide four to six per cent growth, few of us actually get anywhere near this. A study of thousands of ordinary savers found that during a ten year period when shares yielded close to six per cent a year above inflation, savers lost just over one per cent each year. The failure of many of us to capture any real growth is partly due to high charges extracted by the people helping us manage our money. But it's also because most of us don't invest our money particularly well. With financial advisers, unit trust ads and financial journalists forever encouraging us to jump on the latest money-making bandwagon to supposedly 'get better returns', we often rush from one investment to another. Last year emerging markets unit trusts were all the rage. Next year it may be global growth funds, the year after that it could be commodities or European funds or small companies or large companies. If we're brave enough to buy shares, we may be told that telecoms are all the rage, but a year later it's pharmaceuticals and then it could be defensive stocks and after that high-dividend firms and so on and so forth. But each time we or the people managing our savings and pensions are persuaded to jump from one unit trust to another or one share type to another, we pay a shocking price in fees and commissions.

Moreover, while financial market insiders make fortunes when shares shoot up or down, we outsiders often move too late. Because we're not at the centre of the action, news is slow to reach us and so we tend to buy when prices are already too high and panic-sell when they start to fall. Then when you consider all the tricks that insiders play to enrich themselves at our expense – pumping-and-dumping, shorting-and-distorting, pooping-and-scooping, churning-and-burning – you realise that the investment game is heavily rigged against us ordinary savers and only a very few lucky or extremely skilled players will make anything near the returns trumpeted by those who would like to manage our money for us.

If we don't buy unit trusts or shares, then our money can be taken from us through our pension savings. We're encouraged to start saving for a pension as early as possible so that pension fund managers can charge us fees for thirty years or more. Moreover, many pension funds are skimming off several times the fees they tell us they're taking. Even if we're lucky enough to have found a pension scheme which only charges around two per cent a year, over thirty plus years that two per cent a year adds up to a lot of money disappearing into other people's pockets. If our fees are four or five or even six per cent a year for thirty years, unlike our pension fund managers, we're probably not going to make it into the ranks of the super-rich. Another problem is most people don't realise that over £110 billion of their pension savings are in appropriately-named 'zombie funds' – pension funds that are closed to new business and so have no interest whatsoever in attracting new savers. Critics have accused zombie fund managers of just milking them for the maximum in management fees while making little to no effort to get decent returns for savers.

Then there is a neat little trick pension companies like to play on us – the 'switch and get rich'. Financial advisers, journalists and pension scheme sellers sometimes recommend that we switch our pension savings from one company to another by claiming things like we'll get better returns or pay lower costs or find it easier to manage if we consolidate all our pension savings with one provider. If a salesperson can get us to move pension savings of £100,000 from one scheme to another, they can immediately pocket £5,000 or more of our money for themselves – not bad for half an hour's work filling in four or five relatively straightforward forms. When we switch, they get rich.

Plundering pensioners

The people that banks and financial advisers seem to love most are what some in the financial services industry call the 'banana skin and grave brigade' – the elderly who have one foot on a financial banana skin as they don't know much about finance, savings and investments, and the other in the grave as they'll presumably soon be going on to a better place where they won't be needing their money any more, so there's no real harm done relieving them of their cash before they depart. Pensioners and people approaching retirement age have an awful lot more money than younger people. So the finance industry has devised many subtle and not so subtle ways of separating those in their golden years from a significant part of their lifetime savings. The most basic method is by selling them horrifically expensive annuities which pay a pittance in return for customers handing over tens or even hundreds of thousands of pounds to their annuity providers. A nice twist to the annuity story is to convince people to take what's called 'a deferred annuity' – one that doesn't start paying out for five or even ten years. The sales pitch for these is that the longer someone leaves their money untouched, the higher their eventual income will be. Sadly, but not unsurprisingly, many of the elderly people buying these deferred products head off to Cadaver City either before or just a couple of years after their annuities start paying out, leaving most or all of their money in the welcoming hands of the annuity firms.

With bank interest rates so low since the 2007 financial implosion, many pensioners found that their savings were giving them a dismal income. This made it quite easy for financial salespeople to panic them into taking their money out of relatively safe bank and building society accounts and putting it into more colourful and considerably riskier investments. Hundreds of thousands of the elderly were sold supposedly high-income bonds by their banks which tied their money up for five or more years and which had punitive penalties for early withdrawal. Advisers earned hundreds of millions in commissions. But as with deferred annuities, the Grim Reaper carried off quite a few pensioners before their schemes matured. This left the customers' heirs with hefty early exit fees and even huge capital losses when they tried to obtain their inheritances.

Even if a banana-skin-and-graver doesn't have much in the way of ready cash, many will own their own homes. And that too provides enticing opportunities for the ever-inventive financial services industry. Home equity release schemes allow cash-strapped homeowners to top up their pensions a little bit by taking out loans which will be paid back when they eventually sell their homes. These tend to have quite high interest rates. This means that someone aged sixty five taking out a modest £50,000 loan on a home worth £200,000, will find that they owe the whole value of their home by their early to mid eighties. If they later needed money for care home fees or had hoped to pass something on to their children, the fact that they would then get nothing at all for themselves when they sold their home could be a bit of a problem.

Forty one reasons we become poorer

These examples are just the tip of an awfully large and worrying iceberg. The financial services industry has many more ingenious ways of parting us from our cash. As I've tried to make sense of the financial services money-making machine over the last few months, I've definitely and painfully lost my financial virginity and have found at least forty one reasons why much of ordinary people's savings ends up in the pockets of those who are so eager to help us manage our money. You've probably come across many others that I haven't picked up on yet. But hopefully by making readers aware of just some of the different and lucrative ways that ensure financial industry insiders have more money, bigger houses, better cars and more exotic holidays than the rest of us, I might be able to help some people protect their savings against a few of the more imaginative and predatory practices of financial services firms.

When it comes to our money, nobody is on our side – we have to help ourselves.

Good luck.

Part 1

Welcome to the jungle

Reason 1

The financial jungle is a dangerous place

We are living in a Golden Age – for those fortunate enough to work in the financial services industry. For the rest of us, things are not quite so rosy.

Our parents probably had relatively simple financial affairs. Many would have been in long-term jobs with the security of final-salary pensions. So they would have been able to use any extra money to put into the bank, building society, shares or unit trusts as an agreeable add-on to their salaries and pension incomes. If they didn't have the protection of a final-salary scheme, at least they knew that the state could afford to look after them and guarantee a minimum standard of living once they stopped work. All that has changed. People stay in jobs for shorter periods and final-salary pension schemes have all but disappeared in the private sector leaving most of us dependent on our own resources to provide for ourselves and our families. As for governments, many of them can longer afford to look after increasing numbers of pensioners who are living longer. We are pretty much on our own. We have to take full responsibility for our financial futures as employers and governments have all but washed their hands of the task of looking after us.

This has created a massive opportunity for financial services companies whose profits have soared as we have poured our money into bank accounts, unit trusts, investments, pensions and life insurance in our search for some kind of financial security. Unfortunately, as we have increasingly turned to financial services professionals for help managing our money, it's far from clear that the financial services industry has served us well. Instead there has been a long series of financial products mis-selling scandals which have cost ordinary people many tens of billions of pounds and decimated the savings of hundreds of thousands of us.

Deregulation of the pensions industry in the 1980s led to millions of workers in safe, inflation-protected final-salary pension schemes being sold risky investment-based pensions by commission-hungry salespeople using hugely exaggerated projections of the likely investment returns. After a bitter battle lasting years, the industry paid more than £15 billion in compensation. But thousands died before seeing a penny in compensation and tens of thousands more were never compensated and so lost much of their pension income.

In the late 1980s and early 1990s, around five million of us were sold endowment mortgages which would supposedly pay off our mortgages once they matured. Again, salespeople used grossly unrealistic projections of investment returns to lure us into taking these products. When the returns were lower than expected, millions found themselves with large shortfalls which they had to pay off. All in all, endowment mortgage customers had to find about another £40 billion to clear their debts. This time there would be no compensation.

In the mid 1990s, hundreds of thousands of savers put almost £8 billion into high-income bonds. Within the industry these were called 'precipice bonds' due to the way investors would see the value of their savings plummet were the stock market to fall significantly, which it did. Many investors didn't realise that their original capital was at risk and when the bonds matured they found out that their savings had magically evaporated. Retired people, who were encouraged to buy these bonds to boost their pension income, were reported to have been particularly badly hit. Some compensation was paid, but about £5 billion of this money may have been lost while the people selling these products pocketed generous commissions of over £400 million.

At the turn of the millennium the financial services industry had new products in search of suckers. First up were 'guaranteed' stock market investments. These promised to pay anywhere between 80 per cent to 135 per cent of stock-market index growth (depending on the company offering the product) for a five- or six-year period and guaranteed to return all of an investor's capital even if the stock-market index fell a little bit. People put around £10 billion a year into these products. What most savers apparently didn't realise was that over three quarters of the benefits of stock-market investing come from the dividends paid by the companies whose shares are bought and not from any movements in the overall market. Yet these products only paid out on increases in the market index – all the gains from owning the shares were kept by the companies selling these products. Most buyers got back less than they would have earned just leaving their money in an ordinary bank account, but massive profits were made by those selling these schemes.

When savings interest rates collapsed following the 2007 financial crisis, there was a flood of money out of banks as savers searched for higher returns. Thousands of mainly elderly people were targeted by their banks and financial advisers and persuaded to move their savings from reasonably safe deposit accounts into unit trusts and other stock-market investments which were marketed as 'low-risk', 'cautious' and 'balanced' – all fine-sounding, reassuring words. Unfortunately the most widely sold were actually extremely high risk, not at all cautious, highly unbalanced and didn't give any growth. Moreover, they had huge penalties for early withdrawals. There were heartbreaking stories in the press about people in their eighties and even nineties advised to put their life savings into long-term investment plans even though the customers were already near, at or beyond the average life expectancy. Some went on their final journey long before the plans matured and their children were heavily penalised for cashing in before the maturity dates. Many of those who survived lost tens of thousands of pounds. Again, those selling these products made hundreds of millions in commissions.

"Investors again find themselves at the wrong end of an industry that created overly complex, opaque and expensive products that neither they nor their advisers understood or investigated properly."[1]

At the time of writing, several new financial mis-selling scandals are well underway scooping up hundreds of thousands of victims. But it will be a few years before people realise they were bound to lose money by being encouraged to shift their savings into products that had little chance of providing anything like the returns trumpeted by eager bank advisers, financial specialists, tame personal finance journalists and pension-fund sellers.

Our friends tend to talk about their investment successes and to be very quiet about the occasions when they've lost money. So, much of the misery caused by rapacious financial products salespeople goes unnoticed. However, we do sometimes get glimpses of the scale of the problem when the rich and famous or celebrities also fall victims and come a financial cropper. One piece of research identified twenty five top-class athletes from a variety of sports and different countries who between them earned over £356 million during their working lives and yet all had major financial difficulties after their sporting careers were over.[2] And a study in the USA found that seventy eight per cent of NFL players are either broke or have serious financial problems after they retire and about sixty per cent of former NBA players go bust within five years of retirement. Some of these former sports stars were responsible for their own problems through too much drinking, drug-taking, philandering, binge-shopping or other probably enjoyable but expensive and self-destructive hobbies. But the majority lost their money by following appalling financial advice given by self-serving salespeople masquerading as financial experts.

"Within the City you find many who are greedy and

talented, many who are greedy but untalented, but few who are talented but not greedy."[3]

The main problem is that as we have become ever more dependent on financial services professionals to help us with our money, the industry has become increasingly greedy, cynical, short-termist and self-interested. Many savers genuinely believe that banks, financial advisers, insurance companies and fund management firms are offering impartial investment advice. But most financial services staff are just salespeople ordered to sell a small range of products which generate the greatest level of commissions and profits for their employers, or themselves if they are self-employed. We have to realise that apart from a very few rare exceptions, nobody is on the side of ordinary savers. The interests of the professionals are usually diametrically opposed to ours. To maximise their earnings, they have to take as much of our money as they can. Only once we understand that financial services middlemen cannot be trusted and that we have to take full responsibility for our own finances can we have a chance of protecting our money from the industry's predatory behaviour and maybe even get a reasonable return on our savings.

Reason 2

We think three per cent is a small number

Unfortunately, most of us have little idea how much we are paying other people to look after our savings. Even if we were to ask what level of charges we'll be paying for the two most popular investment products - unit trusts and pensions – we'll probably be told that the 'annual management charges' are anywhere between 1.3 per cent and 1.7 per cent. That probably sounds like an acceptably small number. With more complex products like life insurance, investment bonds, with-profits funds, guaranteed bonds, kick-out funds, combination bonds and so on, providers will not usually reveal their charges as they claim they're included in the price of the products.

> **"With traditional with-profits funds, insurance companies can effectively take as much as they like in expenses from the fund. You do not know how much that is."**[4]

However, the 1.3 to 1.7 per cent is usually only the tip of the fees and commissions iceberg. A typical unit trust might have an annual management fee of say 1.5 per cent. But there are also other costs which combine with the management charge to produce what's called the total expense ratio (TER). When these are included, most people will be paying closer to two per cent (see *Reason 24 – We put our trust in unit trusts*). You might think that something called the 'total expense ratio' would cover all the costs. But there are other charges like share dealing (covering brokers' commissions, price effects and bid/offer spreads on shares and bonds bought) which can add another one per cent or more a year to our bills. Then when you take account of the initial cost of purchasing units, which is usually about five per cent, we're probably paying well over three per cent a year to the unit trust fund manager – at least twice the annual management charge which most sellers normally quote.

Similarly, many pension policies will claim that we're only paying about 1.5 per cent a year, with some reducing this to just one per cent a year after ten years. However, here again there are costs which aren't actually included in the annual management charge. For example, anywhere from a quarter to two thirds of our first year's or two years' contributions may be paid directly to the person or organisation which sold us the pension policy rather than into our pension plan. Further, there will be annual management and dealing costs of one per cent to two per cent for the shares, bonds or funds where the pension provider invests our money. So again, it's easy to end up paying three per cent or more each year when we think we're paying less than half that. A lot of older pensions might even be charging us up to six per cent. It doesn't take a mathematical genius to work out that paying four, five or a massive six per cent a year for thirty or more years is not a great way to build up a large pension pot – at least not for the saver.

Gobbling up our money

Now you may still feel that it's not that important if we're actually paying three or four per cent rather than the seemingly modest 1.5 per cent or so usually quoted by most unit trusts and pension companies. After all, both are pretty small numbers. But the problem is that we tend to view the percentages we are being charged against the total of our money. Compared to a hundred per cent, one and a half per cent, or two per cent or even three percent will seem small beer. In reality, the one, two or more likely three per cent is disastrous both for the growth of our savings and often for our initial capital. What we really ought to be doing is comparing the charges we pay to the difference between investing in a unit trust or pension, where there is always some risk of loss, and what we could earn by just leaving our money in the relative safety of a bank account.

Shares and bonds may leap up an exhilarating twenty to thirty per cent in a year or even collapse by a similarly terrifying amount. But over the long term, investments in shares through unit trusts, pensions or other such schemes will tend to give a return of about four to six per cent a year above inflation.

In the forty eight years since the start of the FTSE All-Share Index in 1963, shares have given an average of 11.8 per cent a year. If we knock off inflation of 6.2 per cent a year, the real return on shares drops to 5.6 per cent a year. Had we left our money in cash over the same period, we would have got an 8.5 per cent a year return or a real return of 2.3 per cent a year after deducting inflation. So the benefit of having money in shares, unit trusts or pension funds was just above three per cent a year. If we're paying one and a half or two per cent or even three per cent a year in charges, that will wipe out a large part if not all of our potential earnings from putting our money in a possibly risky investment rather than in a bank account. If we're paying four per cent or more, we're guaranteed only one thing – to lose money.

Say, for example, that over our investing life – the thirty years from about thirty five to sixty five – we hope our investments will grow by £200,000, not an unreasonable sum for anyone saving for a pension. If the £200,000 represents growth of four per cent and we're paying three of those four per cent to the financial services industry, then they get £150,000 of the growth and we get £50,000. Suddenly, three per cent starts looking like an awfully big number. In fact, it can seem like an unacceptably large number as it eats up three quarters of our potential gains. If we're going to get anything at all back from our savings, then we need to get that three per cent down closer to one per cent or even half a per cent (see Figure 1).

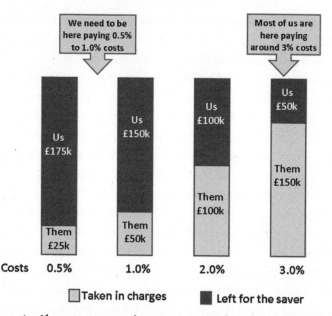

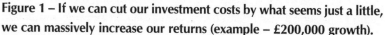

Figure 1 – If we can cut our investment costs by what seems just a little, we can massively increase our returns (example – £200,000 growth).

Were the people keen to get us investing our money to tell us that we could lose at least half, or more probably most, of our potential gains by paying them their fees and commissions, then their products might be rather less attractive, fewer people would be tempted to take a punt with their hard-earned cash and the incomes of financial services insiders would be rather less magnanimous. Hopefully, by the time you've read *Pillaged*, you'll have a few more ideas about how to go from excessive charges of three per cent or more a year to nearer a more acceptable level of one per cent or less.

Playing the percentages game

With many financial products we are not told the real costs. When some costs are disclosed, these are almost never the total costs, whatever salespeople or call centre workers claim to the contrary. Moreover, the costs are almost always expressed in terms of percentages rather than in pounds, dollars or euros. Were we to discover the real-money costs of products like unit trusts, pensions and life insurance, many of us would probably not be quite so eager to hand over our savings. For example, paying around three per cent a year on £50,000 invested in unit trusts doesn't sound nearly as painful as more than £7,500 to £15,000 being pocketed by fund managers over the five-to ten-year period they usually advise us to keep our money in their investments. Or, if we were told up front that a pension fund manager might take a hundred thousand pounds or more from us during the thirty or so years we save for our retirement, we might be tempted to reconsider the wisdom of trusting them with our cash. Using percentages instead of real costs is a bit like casinos making us use plastic chips instead of real money. By having us work with funny money rather than real money, we are not fully aware of the actual amounts that are being taken from us.

So, next time you're with a financial adviser, wealth management planner, bank adviser, insurance consultant, retirement planner or some other kind of financial products salesperson, don't believe that the annual management charge or total expense ratio is all you'll be paying. Instead ask them to list out every single cost that can possibly be taken from the four or five per cent growth that you're likely to get. Then, if you find that the people managing your money are taking most of the growth for themselves, you should probably walk away. In fact, if you already have unit trusts, a pension or some other investments, it might be worth asking the provider the same kinds of questions about the real, not just the published, level of costs and the effects that will have on annual returns of around four to five per cent. You may be surprised by what you discover and find out that it's time to move on and ask someone else to handle your savings.

As for those who work in financial services - they know that three per cent is a very big number indeed. With well over £3.5 trillion of our money in savings, unit trusts and pensions, this three per cent gives them over £105 billion of our money every year - more than £413 million every single working day.

Reason 3

We're influenced by financial journalists and media experts

Journalists have mortgages too

It must be quite difficult being a fashion journalist. There are, I suppose, about four main seasons a year – Spring, Summer, Autumn and Winter. Each season has about thirteen weeks and during those thirteen weeks fashion journalists have to find new and exciting things to write about, thirteen times for each season, to both keep their readers interested and to attract lots of expensive, glossy ads. Of course, most fashion journalists are not really journalists in the sense of reporting something new. They are mainly in the business of pushing the products of those companies which give their employers the most advertising and making sure we keep on buying stuff that's usually hideously overpriced and which we don't need. But perhaps that doesn't really matter as fashion journalism is just a game that cannot seriously damage readers' wealth. If readers are actually foolish enough to believe what the fashion journalists write, their only losses will be a little money spent buying clothes which may make them look slightly ridiculous and which they'll probably not wear more than a couple of times, if at all.

Personal finance journalists are similar to fashion journalists. They too have to find something new and exciting to write about every week. And they must try to push their readers to put their savings into the products which the main advertisers are keen to sell or into shares where the journalists and their associates may have a financial interest. But things become a little more serious when people actually follow the advice of personal finance journalists as readers' losses really can start to hurt their pockets.

"Personal finance is almost as corrupt. ...Financial institutions and PR companies target millions of pounds from marketing budgets at a few dozen business journalists, and almost anything goes. Some journalists boast of lifestyles that are little more than perpetual junkets."[5]

There's an insider joke amongst personal finance journalists that there only are seven different stories they can write and each week they have to dress these seven stories up so they look new, important and interesting.

Personal finance journalists can have an important role to play in helping us with our finances. They can let us know what's happening with stock markets; inform us about new and possibly complex financial products, for example exchange traded funds; explain the tax implications of various investment strategies; direct us to the best places to buy financial services; alert us to some of the most egregious scams and even help out a few readers who are fighting for justice against some incompetent, overly bureaucratic financial institution or other. But like the rest of us, journalists have mortgages to pay, children to educate and a lifestyle to maintain. So they are likely to be more than acquiescent when it comes to keeping the major financial services advertisers happy and unlikely to ever be too critical of the finance industry's greed or dishonesty. We should all read the personal finance pages in our newspapers in order to keep up to date with what is happening. But there are a number of caveats we should bear in mind to ensure that we take most things written by personal finance journalists with a generous helping of scepticism.

- **They're seldom financial experts** – If personal finance journalists were true experts in their field then they would be making millions working for firms like Goldman Sachs or Barclays Wealth Management rather than eking out a rather precarious existence trying to write a weekly column that will satisfy their editors, readers and advertisers. Personal finance journalists will tend to have good socialising skills to maintain a network of people to feed them material and reasonable writing ability to turn that material into compelling stories. But they may not be exactly the kind of people to whom we should entrust our financial futures.

- **They're often puffing, not reporting** – Frequently they will be writing 'puff pieces' praising a product or a company by turning a persistent PR person's press release into something that convincingly masquerades as a news story.

- **It's too late** – By the time we read about the latest investment trend – shares, unit trusts, buy-to-let, guaranteed bonds, emerging markets, small caps, kick-out bonds, combination bonds or whatever – in our weekend newspaper, the financial services insiders have already moved into the market and prices are rising. Once all the suckers read about what's happening, see the gains everyone seems to be making, think about whether to dive in, discuss it with their families, friends and work colleagues and then jump on the bandwagon, prices are probably too high and the bubble is about to burst. The insiders then get out with their profits, prices falter and plunge and the herd get stung yet again.

- **Causing blue-arse-fly behaviour** – Personal finance journalists have to find something new to write about every week. Like fashion journalists, they must keep encouraging their readers to jump on the latest fad, flitting from one type of bank account or fund or investment or market to another – what might be called 'blue-arse-fly money management'. Yet the more people move their savings from one place to another, the more they lose in charges, commissions and fees and thus the less they keep for themselves.

- **Blowing and bursting bubbles** – To keep their readers' attention, journalists will try to sensationalise their stories. So, whether something – house prices, interest rates or stock markets - is stagnant, slightly increasing or slightly falling, the tendency for journalists to describe what is happening in overly vivid colours causes ordinary savers to rush in and out of investments magnifying price movements both up and down and losing us money whether we are buying or selling.

A tip

Some personal finance journalists will go as far as to tip individual shares or unit trusts. On the positive side, personal finance journalists probably know more about what's happening than most of us and so they may be able to guide us towards particular sectors (utilities, energy, pharmaceuticals etc) or companies that are likely to prosper in the near future. Moreover, in many cases merely the fact that a share has been tipped can cause the price to go up seemingly proving that the journalist was enormously prescient.

> **"About two years ago I set up a fake portfolio where I bought 100 shares of each company C....... claimed was a good deal and to date the portfolio has lost huge amounts of money. It's a good thing I didn't use real money and take his advice."**

But readers should tread extremely carefully before taking any tips too seriously. For a start, a journalist may be pushing a share which they or their associates have already bought and which they will sell as soon as the ignorant masses follow the tip and push the price up. Another danger is that tipsters are often horribly wrong. Research in the US suggested that experts advising which mutual funds (called unit trusts in Britain) to choose and which shares to buy achieve around just sixty per cent of the average market growth. Sometimes tipsters can really make a mess of things. In Britain at the start of 2007, *The Times*, *Sunday Times* and *Daily Telegraph* all advised readers to buy shares in the Royal Bank of Scotland (RBS) as they felt it was in the best shape of any of the high street banks. A few months later the RBS was destined to be the largest bankruptcy in British history. In the US, in July 2008 one of the leading business publications predicted 'Lehman won't fail'. On 15 September 2008 Lehman collapsed.

Share tipping is particularly widespread and influential on US television with the main financial shows attracting huge audiences of apparent believers. But one commentator raised the alarm; 'Instead responsible journalism has been replaced by the C......s and K......s put in front of a camera to entertain their misinformed viewers as they advise them on how to best squander their 401ks (pensions savings)'.[6]

You have been warned.

Reason 4

We'll all end up in the 'banana skin and grave brigade'

Siphoning off their savings

The people that banks and financial advisers seem to find most enticing are what some in the financial services industry call the 'banana skin and grave brigade' – elderly people who have one foot on a financial banana skin as they don't know much about finance, savings and investments and the other in the grave as they'll presumably soon be departing this life. As many of the banana skin and grave brigade will have worked all their lives and saved by buying homes, pensions, life insurance, shares and other assets, they tend to control a proportion of national wealth that is much greater than their part of the total population.

But it is not only their wealth which makes the elderly attractive targets. It is also their behaviour and their vulnerability. With most not working, they tend to have the time to listen to financial advisers' sales pitches; they are often more polite than younger prospects and would consider it rude to interrupt or contradict a seller; they are frequently members of social groupings (like bridge clubs, choirs, church groups and voluntary organisations) where sellers can get themselves invited to offer supposedly 'independent' investment advice; they may be lonely or have less human contact than younger working people and so may permit cold-callers to visit them in their homes; and, if fleeced, they are more likely to be too embarrassed or too frightened to complain to regulatory authorities or to take legal action.

"As an older investor you are the top target for con artists. The files of security agencies are filled with tragic examples of senior investors who have been cheated out of their savings and even the equity in their own homes."

Within this group are the ultimate targets for advisers – elderly widows also called 'blue-rinsers'. Although things are changing with more women entering the workforce, for most people currently approaching, at or beyond retirement age, it will still tend to be the man who has handled financial matters and investments. So, widows with savings, equity in their homes and maybe life insurance payments from their husband's death and yet who are relatively financially inexperienced are wrinkly but ripe, juicy targets for financial sellers, both the relatively honest and the more obviously unscrupulous.

The classic approach to selling to the elderly is to use fear. The two things the elderly usually fear most are outliving their savings and becoming so unwell that they have to sell their homes to pay for nursing-home care. This makes them easy targets for advisers with both products like annuities promising guaranteed income and thus peace of mind and with all sorts of more complex investments advertising (but not guaranteeing) high returns. Some sellers use what they call 'FAG selling' ('Fear and Greed' or 'Fear, Anger, Greed') – they exploit older people's fear of lasting longer than their money, their anger at having to worry about money and their greed when offered opportunities to increase their savings.

Many financial advisers specialise in the lucrative market of selling to retirees and those planning their retirement. They can have titles like 'senior wealth advisers', 'retirement planning advisers', 'elder planning specialists' or even the rather scientific-sounding 'financial gerontologist'. There have been numerous investigations where these sellers have been found to have used 'troubling marketing tactics'; 'sophisticated marketing techniques...designed to scare and manipulate seniors into purchasing annuities' and, of course, deliberate lies. One set of dubious products typically sold and mis-sold to the banana-skin-and-gravers were longer-term (five or more years) stock-market investments with punitive penalties for early withdrawal. These were recommended to both men and women in their late seventies and mid eighties when the average life expectancy for men and women was around eighty six. Naturally, quite a few customers with the longer-term stock-market products died before their investments matured and their heirs found that, after deduction of early-withdrawal penalties, the investment companies returned considerably less than had been invested. Others have been sold deferred annuities – these are annuities which guarantee a certain level of income for life, but customers are encouraged to defer withdrawing an income for five or even ten years in order to supposedly allow their capital and thus eventual income to grow. Again, many checked out either before or just after their deferred annuities started to pay out, leaving all their savings in the hands of the annuity companies and nothing at all for their heirs.

One of the possibly more gruesome selling scams targeting mostly the elderly is the 'reload' scam, also called 'double dipping'. Here an adviser gets a prospect to move their capital into a high-risk stock-market fund. If the fund value falls, substantially reducing the target's capital, another adviser from the same company contacts the prospect offering new, exciting investment opportunities which will supposedly not only recoup the lost capital, but even increase it above what was originally invested. Of course these promises can seldom be met. But by convincing the investor to move their money again to another product, the adviser profits from another lot of large upfront fees giving the firm of advisers two lucrative bites of the banana-skin-and-graver's ever-shrinking cherry.

Farewell, home sweet home

If the elderly don't have much ready cash available, that hasn't deterred eager financial sellers. Although some over-65s may have limited pensions and savings, many own their own homes making them what's called 'asset-rich but cash-poor'. Seeing the potential of the asset-rich cash-poor market, financial firms have devised various schemes, often called 'equity release', which promise to free up some or all of the value in their customers' homes allowing them to live more comfortably till they die in return for the firms taking part or whole ownership of their customers' properties. But as these products tend to be extremely lucrative for their providers and sellers, they risk being less than wonderful for the people lured into taking them. There are two main types of equity release scheme – loans based on the value of the home and sale and rent back.

There are various commonly-sold schemes where customers can get either a lump sum or regular income by taking out a loan which is set against the value of their homes. When their home is sold because they either move into a care home or go directly to meet their Maker, the loan plus interest has to be paid back. Interest rates on these loans tend to be significantly higher than those offered to a younger person taking a mortgage to buy a property. So, thanks to the wonders of compound interest, even sums that appear quite modest when originally borrowed can turn into massive debts after a few years. For example, someone aged sixty five borrowing £50,000 at seven percent interest against a home worth £200,000 would find their debt to the lender had shot up to about £100,000 after ten years and £200,000 – the total value of their home – by the time they hit eighty five (see Figure 1).

Age	5% a year	7% a year	9% a year
65	£50,000	£50,000	£50,000
70	£69,814	£70,128	£76,931
75	£81,444	£98,358	£118,368
80	£103,946	£137,951	£182,124
85	£132,665	£193,484	£280,220
90	£169,318	£271,371	£431,154

Figure 1 – Even a small £50,000 equity release loan taken out at age 65 can turn into a massive debt within the borrower's lifetime.

If they lived longer, they would find that a loan which originally represented just a quarter of their home's value could even exceed the total worth of their home by the time they move on to a better place. Though after a series of scandals, a lot of schemes now guarantee that a customer's debt cannot exceed the value of their home. Many people may decide for health or other reasons to sell their home after ten to fifteen years, thus before their equity release loan has exceeded the value of their home. But even if their equity release loan is less than the value of their home when they sell it, they may find that they have so little money left after repaying their loan that they are unable to afford to buy a retirement home or pay care-home costs. Numerous stories suggest that people selling these products are failing to inform their prospects of the serious risks of them being rapidly impoverished when persuaded to take one of these loans.

"The only winners in equity release are the companies and elderly people who die just a few years after taking out the policy."

An even more worrying development is the way sellers have encouraged tens of thousands of people, most of them elderly, into sale and rent back contracts. With sale and rent back, a homeowner sells part or all of their property. Depending on their agreement, they can then live in their homes either rent-free, at a low rent or paying full market rent. There are several problems with sale and rent back. Firstly, the providers only pay about sixty to seventy five per cent of a property's market value. Moreover, there have been cases where the contracts only gave customers short-term tenancy rights. This made it easy for the companies which have bought the homes to force their tenants out by raising the rent to unsustainable levels so that the occupants had to leave. Then the buyer could resell the property for a very healthy profit. There can also be terms in the contract, for example around the annual maintenance which the tenant must carry out, which give the buyer another way of finding a legal loophole to evict tenants to gain possession of the property. And, of course, if a person becomes ill or pops their clogs shortly after taking out a sale or rent back agreement, the finance company has got hold of the property at well below its real market price.

Reason 5

The finance industry is out of control

Much, probably too much, has already been written and will continue to be written about the current financial crisis. The various well-paid experts seem eager to tell us what happened, who was to blame and what needs to be done to avoid a reoccurrence. Unfortunately not all their outpourings have been enormously useful as most of them failed to predict the collapse, failed to understand what was happening at the time and failed to change their opinions one iota in the light of what happened. Given the many millions of words already expended by the legions of pundits, it would be difficult to add a lot to the debate in just a few pages here. However, it is worth spending just a few minutes tracing some key developments of the last few years that have allowed the finance industry almost unlimited access to our money and the power to siphon off as much as it wants.

From socially useful to socially destructive

The activities performed by the main financial institutions and the ways they make their profits have changed dramatically in the last thirty to forty years. To hugely simplify what is obviously a much more complex picture, we could divide the finance industry's activities into three main types:

- **retail services** – offering savings accounts, mortgages, credit cards and small business loans

- **supporting the economy** – providing money for corporate investment, financing international trade and assisting mergers and acquisitions
- **proprietary trading** – speculating in shares, commodities, futures and foreign exchange and developing complex financial products to sell to the unit trusts and pensions funds which manage our money

Retail services are socially useful as they enable us to manage our finances and buy our homes and they help our small businesses thrive. Supporting the economy is useful as it allows wealth creation through businesses and trade developing goods, services and jobs. However, proprietary trading usually consists of what is called 'rent seeking' – extracting profits for financial institutions by churning our money from one product to another without creating any value for savers, for the economy or for society as a whole.

"If financial markets work properly, they help the economy to prosper: if they fail to provide financing for worthwhile capital projects, if they divert money to the worthless objects of speculative bubbles and fads, they are a hindrance to the economy."[7]

In fact, rent-seeking can be seen as socially destructive because it depletes our savings, reduces the money available to finance economic growth and harms social cohesion by increasing the gap between wealthy finance industry insiders and the rest of us. However, rent-seeking is vastly more profitable than retail services and supporting the economy. So, over the last few years, many of the main financial firms have vastly grown their proprietary trading operations at the expense of their much less lucrative but socially and economically useful activities (see Figure 1).

The extent of this shift from providing social and economic value to purely extracting profits from our money for themselves could be seen when the main banks announced their 2009/2010 results. In spite of substantially reducing lending to homebuyers and businesses, in some cases cutting it by half, most banks managed to make record profits. Meanwhile hundreds of thousands of their customers lost their homes, tens of thousands of businesses collapsed due to a lack of funding, millions became unemployed and tens of millions of ordinary people saw the value of their savings and pensions depleted.

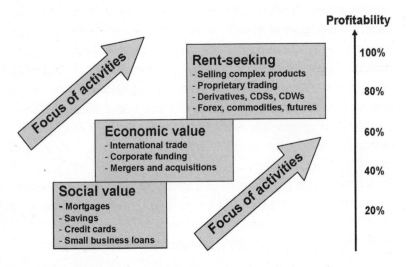

Figure 1 – Many financial institutions have moved from socially and economically useful activities to much more profitable proprietary trading.

In a world of their own

As financial institutions have drifted away from less profitable but socially and economically useful activities to highly profitable trading and speculation, a huge gap has opened up between the level of financial activity carried out by the finance industry and what is happening in the real economy. There are plenty of figures which show this. For example, in the 1970s foreign exchange trading was worth eleven times the value of global trade, by 2010 this had shot up to seventy times. Over the same period, trading in oil futures went from only a fifth of the value of global production to ten times global production. And credit default swaps (insurance policies taken out against risky loans) exploded from $8 trillion in 2004 to almost $60 trillion by 2007, making this market worth more than the total gross domestic product (GDP) of all the main countries in the world (about $55 trillion).

This extraordinary growth in financial activities without any corresponding growth in real economic activity has led to what has been called 'the financialisation' of our society. There is a huge amount of financial activity taking place which is massively profitable for financial institutions but is completely disconnected from what is happening in the real economy of producing and selling goods and services. It's estimated that only about a tenth of foreign exchange activity is related to real businesses exporting and importing. Ninety per cent is just speculation by financial institutions. Worse still, this financialisation can cause repeated economic instability leading to job losses, widespread impoverishment and political upheaval as enormous speculative bets placed by financial institutions against countries, currencies or major corporations mean that now it is often more profitable for financiers to wreck the targets of their speculation to make short-term profits than to promote long-term global development and wealth creation. In the last few years we've seen many examples of the prices of commodities like oil and metals being pushed up due to speculation and market manipulation by financial institutions, rather than due to any increase in demand from the real economy. In the next five to ten years, as the world's population increases and food production struggles to keep up with demand, we can expect this massive speculation to move to food products. This will drive up prices, cause food shortages, lead to tens of thousands of deaths from malnutrition and associated diseases and even cause political turmoil in many poorer countries. But the finance industry will make hundreds of billions in profits for a few lucky insiders at the expense of the vast majority of us outsiders in what multimillionaire traders laughingly call 'financial mass murder'.

The TBTF extortion

In the 1960s, the total balance sheets of all Britain's banks were worth just a third of the country's gross domestic product. Our banks have grown so fast compared to all other sectors of our economy that today they have balance sheets that are five times our GDP. Just before the 2007 crash, RBS had potential liabilities of £1.9 trillion. So a single bank had liabilities that were well in excess of Britain's £1.4 trillion GDP. Barclays at £1.2 trillion and the Lloyds Group at £1 trillion were each close to GDP. On just a few of its many atrocious deals, RBS lost more money than our country spends on things like defence or education. HBOS (taken over by Lloyds) performed a similar remarkable feat with many of its property investments. Naturally, after the big bailout all those involved got huge bonuses and many walked away from the smoking rubble of their own avarice and incompetence to live the life of multimillionaires at British taxpayers' and savers' expense.

The massive growth of our banks and other financial institutions like the US insurance behemoth AIG, has led to what's been called the 'too big to fail (TBTF) syndrome'. Our financial institutions are now so huge that if they make enormous losses due to their greed and stupidity, they can blackmail politicians into handing over our money to bail them out by threatening that the financial system will be wrecked if they are allowed to collapse. It is far from obvious that this is or was ever true. In fact, the economy might have been a lot better off today if several of the main banks had been allowed to go to the wall, their management teams sacked without any compensation and then they were reconstituted with new leadership. Moreover, dragging a few leading bankers before the courts for corruption, insider trading, misleading shareholders, negligence and breach of fiduciary duties might have helped clear the air. However, political leaders across the world rely on generous cash handouts from the finance industry and their lobbyists to keep them in power and finance their election activities. So the interests of ordinary savers and taxpayers were sacrificed to keep the financiers in the luxury to which they had become accustomed.

If I ruled the world

Following the 1929 Wall Street Crash and ensuing depression, US president Franklin D. Roosevelt signed the Glass-Steagall Act into law in 1933. Amongst other reforms of the financial sector, the Act split what has been called 'utility banking' or 'commercial banking' – taking deposits from ordinary savers and mortgage lending – from what has been caricatured, not always unfairly, as 'casino banking' – investment banking and financial speculation. The underlying idea was that ordinary savers' money, which is largely insured by governments (and thus taxpayers), should not be put at risk by banks' rent-seeking speculative activities. Under pressure from the finance industry, the provisions of the Act were gradually watered down until it was fully repealed in 1999. There are good reasons to believe that the financial mayhem of the last few years has been in large part due to the repeal of Glass-Steagall.

There have been calls for the reintroduction of the Act or some similar provision again separating deposit-taking from speculative activity. But while bleating helplessly about the need for banks to lend to homebuyers and businesses, today's political pygmies in the US, EU and Britain have been afraid to defend the interests of ordinary citizens and so have avoided taking on the finance industry. Instead, the financial institutions have managed to use their massive resources to pay off our politicians and the few half-hearted reforms that have been adopted have been so feeble that they led to a big jump in the price of bank shares as investors realised that banks' profitability would not be affected. In the US in early 2010,

Republican politicians were reportedly doing the rounds of financial institutions offering to block reforms of the financial system in return for healthy donations to their funds for re-election in November 2010. One senator who vigorously backed the Wall Street bailout and then opposed reforms was accused of 'unabashedly courting Wall Street bankers for political money, happy to scratch their backs if they'll scratch his.'[8]

Meanwhile, Wall Street lobbyists were putting pressure on the Senate Banking Committee claiming that any reforms would 'lead to serious unforeseen (and unforeseeable) consequences that will inhibit job creation, endanger the ongoing economic recovery, and prevent the American economy from reaching its full potential'.[9] Perhaps it slipped their minds that it was the self-serving excesses of a largely out-of-control finance industry which had caused job losses and the recession in the first place.

Our leading financial institutions have pulled off a remarkable coup. They have extracted extraordinary amounts of money from us through risk-taking, gambling, corruption, speculation and fraud. When things went belly up, they blackmailed governments into rescuing them with our money, while they got rid of all their dud investments by handing them over to taxpayers. Then they revalued their remaining investments creating enormous paper profits and paid most of those profits to their senior staff in huge salaries and bonuses rather than passing them back to their main shareholders – the unit trusts and pension funds which look after our savings and the taxpayers whose money rescued them. And now that they have effectively emasculated our political leaders using bribes and threats, financial institutions find it more rewarding to siphon off our savings through highly profitable rent-seeking speculation rather than spending too much effort on more socially and economically useful, but less lucrative, activities like lending to consumers and businesses. The finance industry truly seems to rule the world and there's nothing either we or our fill-their-own-pockets, self-serving, Lilliputian leaders can do about it.

Reason 6

Regulators don't regulate

The timid and the toothless

If our elected rulers won't protect us against the greed of a predatory financial services industry, then our last line of defence is probably our financial regulators. Regulators on both sides of the Atlantic all seem to have done well for themselves in the lead up to the financial crisis and its aftermath. But it's far from obvious that they did much for ordinary savers, taxpayers and investors – the people whose interests the regulators were so handsomely paid to defend.

The FSA fiasco

In Britain the main financial regulator the Financial Services Authority (FSA) really boomed with the boom. In 1997 it had a modest annual budget of just £21 million. By 2007, at the height of the boom this had shot up to around £300 million a year. But when the bust came, the FSA party seemed to continue unchecked as its spending leapt up again to over £400 million a year. The FSA pays the highest salaries of any of our many regulators with its boss earning over £600,000 and scores of others on six-figure salaries. Not content with lavishing generous salaries on its staff, the FSA also felt that they deserved bonuses for all their sterling work. In 2007/8, the year the crisis hit, the FSA paid £13.9 million in bonuses. The following year bonuses increased by over forty per cent to £19.7 million. In the latest year for which figures are available, 2009/10, FSA bonuses went up again though this time only by about twelve per cent to £22 million. FSA bosses gave us all the usual excuses for rewarding inaction and incompetence – 'need to attract the best staff', 'excellent work done under difficult conditions' and so on and so forth. But one insider let the cat out of the bag when he admitted, 'Just about everyone in the building got a bonus. The targets were not exactly challenging. You had to be incompetent not to get an award.'[10] But this person was probably being too positive about the situation – in fact, even the utterly incompetent got bonuses.

Not everyone was quite as impressed with the FSA's performance as they were themselves. Following the FSA's inability to spot or prevent the greatest and most expensive banking crisis in British history, one MP accused an FSA boss of being 'not asleep, but comatose'.[11] The head of the FSA did admit that his organisation could have done a slightly better job, 'We are sorry that our supervision did not achieve all it should have done.' But this was a bit like the captain of the Titanic saying, 'we apologise for any turbulence during our voyage and look forward to welcoming you all back aboard the Titanic again soon.'

In the wake of the meltdown which cost us savers and taxpayers many tens of billions, the government brought in several City worthies to propose ways of reforming the financial system. But all these individuals had previously held senior positions at financial institutions which had been found to be involved in lying to savers, defrauding investors, 'siphoning short-term profits from mutual funds', manipulating commodity markets and selling illegal tax avoidance schemes. Unsurprisingly, as they took up their new responsibilities they all professed to be born-again believers in improved regulation to protect ordinary savers and taxpayers from the excesses of the finance industry. But by the time they had finished their expensive deliberations, they ended up seemingly forgetting about our interests and instead warned that excessive regulation could harm London's thriving financial services industry and damage the economy, or at least what little was left of it after the crash caused by greed and excess in the largely unregulated financial services industry. To appease public anger at the City, the government promised a big clampdown on the financial sector, but little to nothing happened except for some half-hearted and futile appeals to financial services bosses not to give themselves massive pay rises and multi-million pound bonuses. Naturally, the all-powerful finance chiefs laughingly ignored our impotent government's entreaties and even executives and senior staff in bankrupted banks saved by taxpayers' money decided they also deserved billions in bonuses.

The new British government has decided to abolish the FSA and transfer its powers for economic management to the Bank of England. This may not exactly be good news for us. The former Deputy Governor at the Bank of England responsible for the stability of the financial system during the crisis was described as being 'asleep in the back shop while there was a mugging out front'.[12] There's no evidence that his successor will be any more vigilant. The FSA's consumer protection activities will be passed to a new Consumer Protection and Markets Authority. But we risk seeing the same people, who have singularly failed to protect us so far, moving into new well-paid jobs where they can continue their dismal performance. Who knows, maybe many of them will even be given huge redundancy packages paid for by us as they leave the FSA to take up their new jobs at the Consumer Protection and Markets Authority? After all, in Britain's public sector, failure has never been an obstacle to excessive rewards and regular advancement. In fact, sometimes it seems that it may be a precondition.

Utterly US-less

As far as regulation of the financial services industry was concerned, things weren't so hot on the other side of the Atlantic either. There was public outrage after the crash when it was revealed that the many US financial regulators had also been paying their staff record levels of bonuses. As in Britain, the heads of the US regulators justified these bonuses for 'superior' performance with excuses like 'the need to recruit and retain the very best people' and 'reward those who worked so hard and showed such great professionalism throughout the crisis.' In making such statements, perhaps the bosses forgot that if they and their staff had bothered to do their jobs properly in the first place, there would not have been a crisis. Moreover, subsequent investigations into the failure of almost two hundred US banks showed that regulators had been guilty of recidivist laziness and incompetence.

> **"We've got a very comfortable equilibrium here where Wall Street praises the authorities and the authorities give Wall Street more or less what it wants. Taxpayers must protect themselves against two things: the corrupting influence of bureaucratic self-interest amongst regulators and the political clout wielded by the large institutions they are supposed to police."**[13]

Anger at US regulators reached a new intensity when it was found that at the height of the crisis, thirty one employees at the Securities and Exchange Commission (SEC) had felt that they had so little work to do that they spent hours each day surfing porn sites and downloading hard-core pornography. One SEC accountant had spent eight hours a day looking at Internet porn and another had accessed porn websites 1,800 times in just two weeks. Although those involved were less than one per cent of the SEC's 3,500 employees, this incident didn't exactly give a flattering impression of the SEC's abilities and dedication to public service.

US regulators appear to have made at least three fatal mistakes. Firstly, there were too many regulators for banks – the Federal

Deposit Insurance Corp (FDIC), Office of the Comptroller of the Currency (OCC) and the Office of Thrift Supervision (OTS). These bodies were funded by the banks they were meant to regulate leading to a situation where the regulators were competing for business with each of them treating the banks more leniently than the other. This was hardly likely to result in effective regulation.

Secondly, regulators failed to respond to the massive growth in products that were developed and sold in markets that were neither transparent nor regulated. These included such things like hedge funds, off-balance sheet structured-investment vehicles, opaque derivatives, collateralized debt obligations and credit default swaps. By 2007, this unregulated 'shadow banking' system was worth about $10 trillion – about the same as all the assets in the main US banking system. It was the collapse of this shadow banking system in 2007 which almost brought down the whole financial system and led to the subsequent crisis and recession.

Thirdly, in addition to the three banking regulators fighting each other, two of the key regulators, the Federal Reserve Board (FRB) and the SEC were engaged in a turf war where they withheld important information from each other. For example, the FRB didn't inform the SEC of a $7 billion shortfall in Lehman's liquidity.

In mid 2010, Congress passed new legislation, the Dodd-Frank bill, aimed at improving regulation of the finance industry. But critics have claimed it has been so watered down by Republican opposition that it fails to deal with key problems like the shadow banking system and the too-big-to-fail issue. Moreover, it gives greater power to the regulators who have repeatedly failed to regulate and still leaves the taxpayer on the hook to bail out financial institutions when the next crisis hits.

"The Dodd-Frank bill places protecting government employees over protecting both the taxpayer and our financial system. At a time when millions of Americans have lost their jobs, generally by no fault

of their own, protecting the jobs of failed bank regulators only adds insult to injury."[14]

If we're really expecting our numerous well-paid regulators to regulate the financial services industry in the interests of ordinary people, we may be profoundly disappointed. As one commentator explained, 'the only result is that when the next mania and panic arrive, and they will, Congress and the regulators will claim they were all someone else's fault.'[15]

It looks like we're on our own and the financial jungle is a dangerous place.

Part 2

Slashing our savings

Reason 7

We're mad enough to save while we owe money

The most common mistake many people make, which impoverishes them while enriching the fortunate people in the finance industry, is probably the easiest to avoid. If we look at the various ways we can borrow or save money, it becomes obvious that we pay much more interest on money that we borrow on store cards, credit cards, overdrafts and home loans than we generally get in interest or growth on money we save in bank accounts, pensions, shares or unit trusts (see Figure 1).

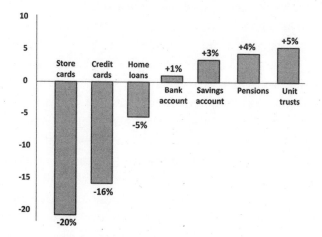

Figure 1 – Some of us save money at low rates of return while at the same time owing money at much higher rates of interest

What this simple example hopefully shows is that millions of people are borrowing money at usurious rates – possibly over twenty per cent on store cards and at least sixteen per cent on credit cards while holding money in bank accounts earning probably less than one per cent. Some of these people may even be investing in a pension or the stock market where they will be lucky if they can gain four to five per cent a year yet they are paying four times that much on unpaid balances on store cards and credit cards. This is clearly complete madness.

The mistake of saving in bank accounts, pensions and shares at paltry rates of interest and growth while paying extraordinary rates on store and credit cards may only be made by a few people. However, a much more common error is where people paying off mortgages are also investing in shares, unit trusts and personal pensions. If you take out a twenty to twenty-five year mortgage for say £200,000, you're going to end up paying somewhere around £400,000 assuming a mortgage rate of about six per cent. If you have £10,000 in savings you could get about £300 a year in a long-term bank deposit account, £400 a year in your pension or £500 a year in a unit trust, but you could save over £600 a year by using this money to pay off your mortgage faster and earlier. For example, if you could pay off an extra £2,000 a year in the first five years of your mortgage, you'd probably be able to reduce your payment time by about three years and cut your interest costs by something in the region of £20,000. That's a much better return than you'll get from most savings or investments, whatever your bank, financial adviser or unit trust salesperson claims about the potential growth of whatever they're keen to flog you.

Of course, in many countries there are tax advantages in saving for a pension. But even taking account of these, you'd have to be getting around forty per cent added on to your pension savings by the taxman to make it worth your while saving in a pension rather than paying off your home loan.

You could argue that in spite of the fact that over the long term pensions have never really returned more than four per cent a year and stock-market investments have only reached around five per cent a year, your particular pension, stock-market or unit trust investments will perform much better than the average punter's and so for you it's worth investing while still owing money on your home. That's an argument I'll deal with in *Part 3 Investing – our pain, others' gain?* However, if you're tempted to think that your investing skills will allow you to outperform the average, please note that here I've taken the long-term return for pensions and shares without deducting any management charges, share dealing costs, sales commissions, upfront fees, early withdrawal penalties and all the other ways finance professionals siphon off our money. Once you take these expenses into account, the strange madness that makes people invest to gain one or two per cent a year while borrowing six figure sums at six per cent or more becomes even more incomprehensible.

As with any comments about where people should put their money, each individual should do their own calculation to see whether they personally should be saving at low rates of return while at the same time paying off borrowing at much higher interest rates. But for hundreds of millions of people around the world, the strange lunacy of borrowing expensively while saving for paltry returns could easily be cured by the application of some elementary arithmetic and just a little common sense.

Reason 8

Few of us have developed our Financial Intelligence

The importance of Financial Intelligence

Over time, our view of human intelligence has developed as society and the demands placed on us have changed (see Figure 1).

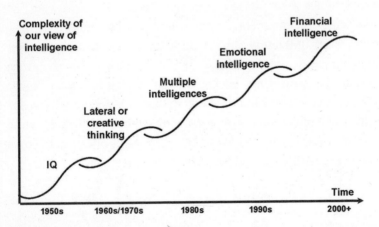

Figure 1 – Our view of intelligence has evolved as we have needed different skills to deal with life's changing challenges

Probably the best-known test of intelligence is the IQ test, developed by French psychologist Binet towards the end of the nineteenth century. He realised that most of the children who went on to higher education came from privileged backgrounds. IQ tests were designed to help children from poorer homes by identifying children's intelligence level whatever their social class. The next major advance was in the 1960s and came from proponents of what has been called lateral (or creative) thinking. Understanding that the human brain is split into two main hemispheres – the left generally associated with analytical and mathematical functions and the right seen as the source of humour, creativity and emotional expression – they criticised the traditional view of intelligence and education for being too limited and sought to expand our understanding of intelligence by teaching lateral thinking techniques such as brainstorming, associative thinking and mind-mapping.

In a groundbreaking book published in the 1980s, author Howard Gardner proposed that we have eight types of intelligence (see Figure 2).

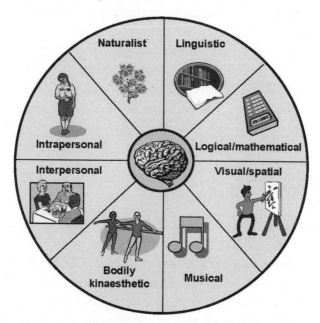

Figure 2 – Gardner's eight types of intelligence

Unfortunately the education systems in too many countries limit themselves to teaching and assessing a limited range of children's different intelligences and many people leave education without developing to their full potential.

As organisations became less hierarchical and we increasingly had to work by cooperating with others through teams and networks rather than just obeying a boss's orders, the idea of emotional intelligence became popular. The basic idea was that in order to effectively work with and through others in networks rather than hierarchies, people needed a high level of emotional intelligence (their EQ) – the ability to understand and master their own emotions, to understand others and to interact with others – as well as a reasonable IQ.

We are now moving into an era where we have to be financially self-reliant, because neither employers nor the state can afford to look after us, and where financial services providers are developing ever more complex and profitable products to sell to us. In this new environment, much is being written about the need to help people adapt by developing their financial intelligence (also called financial literacy) – the ability to do financial planning, make a budget, understand interest rates and compare products that are so complicated that many have twenty to thirty pages of gobbledygook – almost impenetrable legalistic terms and conditions – as part of the sales agreement.

Ignorance isn't bliss

Research across the world has shown that many of us have a worryingly low level of financial intelligence. In one survey, over eighty per cent of people approaching retirement couldn't work out how much a person would have in a bank account after two years if they earned interest at twenty per cent a year. Credit cards make around eighty per cent of their profits from people not paying off their accounts at the end of each month even though it should be more than blindingly obvious that with fifteen to twenty per cent interest rates, credit cards are almost the most expensive way to borrow money. Most people tested didn't realise that they could end up paying much more for a home loan with lower payments over twenty years than they would for one with higher payments over fifteen years; the majority didn't understand compound interest; and almost a quarter couldn't work out basic percentages.

"It is hard to overestimate the extent of financial illiteracy amongst some consumers.....Half of investors do not understand the difference between equities and bonds....Many pension and endowment policy holders did not realise their money was invested in the stock market."[16]

There was even a survey which revealed that the majority of respondents found choosing a financial product like life insurance, a mortgage or a pension more stressful than going to the dentist. Yet these are precisely the people at whom the financial services industry is targeting ever more complex products like high income bonds, kick-out bonds, guaranteed-return stock-market plans, combination bonds, sector-specific unit trusts, hedge-fund funds of funds, commodity funds, highly hazardous foreign exchange trading and extremely toxic and risky spread betting.

Making the wrong decision

Faced with the choice overload of hundreds of different life insurance policies, home loan options and pension plans and thousands of bank accounts and unit trusts, many people feel overwhelmed and have difficulty making the right product choice. About eighty three per cent of people in one study chose the products offered by the best known companies even though these were often much more expensive and considerably less generous than other available options. One of the best known brands in Britain, for example, can charge over three times what competitors charge for its index-tracker unit trust purely because people are familiar with the company name.

One of the greatest failures of people's financial intelligence came with the sale in the US of Adjustable Rate Mortgages (ARMs) – mortgages with low monthly payments for the first few years. These were originally excellent products designed for a very small market niche - trainee lawyers and doctors whose income would increase rapidly once they moved up in their careers. But ARMs were pushed by commission-hungry salespeople to the mass market where people who could afford the initial payments had no chance of being able to make the much higher costs that kicked in after a couple of years. Clearly, most consumers had little understanding of what they were being sold and defaulted when their costs rocketed. By the time the truth hit home, the mortgages had been packaged up, given top-level scores by the ever compliant ratings agencies and sold on to supposedly sophisticated financial institutions which seemingly also hadn't a clue about what they were so eagerly buying.

When buying a financial product, many of us make the fatal mistake of abdicating responsibility to a person whose interests may be diametrically opposed to our own. So we ask our bank savings adviser, insurance agent, pension consultant, mortgage specialist or financial planner to recommend a product and then we accept their recommendation, completely failing to realise that they'll probably propose the one that makes them the highest commission and therefore will probably either be the most expensive for us or else give us the lowest returns. Similarly, when buying up packaged mortgage products many banks and pension funds holding our money trusted the ratings agencies without thinking through that the agencies were mainly interested in maximising their profits by being more than generous in throwing around triple A's like confetti at a mass wedding. People selling financial products are experts at getting us to trust them. As one salesman explained, 'You don't lie to your client, but you make them feel like you're their best friend'. Only by developing our financial intelligence to understand the motivation of those selling financial products and the true nature of those products can we avoid being taken for suckers.

To teach or not to teach?

You could argue that it is the responsibility of parents to teach their children about money. The problem with this view is that it risks perpetuating disadvantage and poverty – people who are poor at financial management are unlikely to be able to pass good money-management skills on to the next generation. So there is a strong case for insisting that schools should put all children aged perhaps fifteen or over through a basic course in financial literacy to give them a grounding in how the financial industry works, how it generates its profits, the kinds of products it sells, how to budget and so on. In theory, the greater our financial intelligence, the more likely we are to make better financial decisions throughout our lives.

However, some experts have suggested that there is little point trying to teach financial skills as no ordinary consumer will ever be able to master the complexity of many of today's financial products or see through the selling tactics of those pushing such products. Several studies have found that people trained in the basics of finance often made worse decisions than those who weren't. The problem is that a little knowledge can be a bad thing – people with some training had the illusion of knowledge and became overconfident in their own abilities. There is also evidence that victims of financial fraud tend to have a higher level of knowledge than the average person. In the US, doctors have been revealed to be some of the worst dupes in falling for dubious investment schemes precisely because their many years of training and the nature of their job made them confident in their own abilities to make correct judgements.

But looking at the frighteningly low level of many people's financial intelligence and the horrific amounts of debt which many young people have taken on, it does seem more than urgent for us to make the effort to rapidly raise our own and our children's levels of financial knowledge otherwise we will continue to become poorer as those in financial services further enrich themselves at our expense.

Reason 9

We don't have Emotional Discipline

How emotionally disciplined are you?

Here are a few questions we should all ask ourselves:

- If our savings are earning very little interest, our pension funds don't seem to be growing and a lot of our friends are talking about how much money they're making from owning a couple of buy-to-let flats, do we decide that we too should jump into the buy-to-let business?
- If we want to put some money into a unit trust, do we choose a top performing fund that's been recommended to us by a financial adviser or that we've recently seen advertised in the personal finance pages of our favourite Saturday or Sunday newspaper?
- If we buy some shares and they lose over thirty per cent of their value, do we sell them to get some money back or hold on for the long term in the hope they'll go up again?
- If the stock market has just crashed and all the press pundits are predicting doom and gloom, do we dive in and put our savings into shares and unit trusts or do we wait till things improve and prices are going up again?
- If interest rates from our bank are derisory and a financial adviser at the bank tells us that most other people are moving their money to the bank's new guaranteed investment bond, do we feel that we've no option but to

do what everyone else seems to be doing?

Buying shares or shampoo

When we invest in shares, put money in unit trusts or purchase a buy-to-let property we are usually acquiring two things – the basic asset and the income that asset will produce either in dividends or rent. Therefore the less we pay for the asset, the better value we are getting and the more likely we are to emerge with a profit. Buying shares or property or any other asset should be like buying shampoo. When prices are low – for example there's a three-for-the-price-of-two offer – we should stock up. When prices are high, we should try to delay buying or search around for another product or brand which is on sale at a lower price. This is why experts say that the only way to make money is to 'buy low, sell high' – buy something (shares, property, art or whatever) when it is out of favour and prices are low and sell when everyone else likes what you've bought and prices shoot up. But most of us do the opposite – we buy high and sell low. When everyone else is rushing into shares, investment bonds, buy-to-lets and so on, we join the crowd not realising that we're probably buying at a time when prices are too high. Then when the smart money gets out and there is a collapse in price, many of us will rush for the exits and sell, possibly even making a loss, only to put our money into the next hot thing when it is also already over-priced.

To 'buy low, sell high' means buying shares or property when prices are crashing and then selling when prices are on the way up. This requires almost superhuman self-control. Most research of investor behaviour has shown that very few of us have this kind of emotional discipline. We're constantly hearing from personal finance journalists how we can earn six per cent or eight per cent a year from putting our money in the stock market. Although theoretically true, most of us will never get anything like this. One of the more recent studies of investor returns in US markets from 1989 to 2008, found that while the annual returns from mutual funds (unit trusts) was

8.35 per cent, most ordinary investors only made a pathetic 1.87 per cent before inflation, giving a loss of just over one per cent after taking account of inflation (see Figure 1).

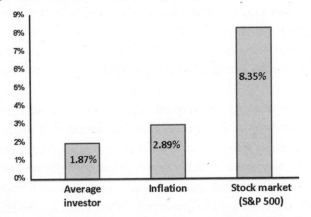

Figure 1 – Ordinary savers seem to earn much less than the overall market because they don't have the emotional discipline to be successful investors

Similar studies in Britain suggested that most savers only gained about one per cent a year, making a loss once inflation was taken into account.

The main reason why most investors actually saw their savings fall in value, while they should have made money, was that they constantly bought too high and sold too low. For example, if everyone else was rushing into say emerging markets or oil & gas or banking stocks, they joined the herd and ended up buying when the price was inflated. Similarly if a sector was out of favour and prices were low, investors would avoid that sector. When some unit trusts shot up and advertised their stellar results, ordinary savers would throw their money into those funds. When other unit trusts collapsed and savers saw their friends making money from better performing investments, many savers would decide to cut their losses and follow the example of those who seemed to have made wiser use of their money. But by rushing into supposedly successful investments, the latecomers would once again end up 'buying high' – buying when prices were inflated by those investments' popularity.

"Emotion and inflation are the greatest destroyers of people's savings."[17]

Why can't we control our emotions?

Most people would probably accept the rational argument that you make money by buying when prices are low and selling when prices are high and, of course you lose your money and your shirt by buying at a high price and selling at a lower price. Yet too many of us fall into the 'buy high, sell low trap'. There seem to be several reasons why we fail to make best use of our savings:

- **We follow the herd** – When journalists, investment pundits, friends or work colleagues gush about how easy it is to make money by buying gold, emerging markets funds, buy-to-lets, guaranteed investment bonds or whatever is fashionable at the time, we join in the rush of the Gadarene Swine not realising that by the time something has become the subject of water-cooler or dinner-party conversations and even accepted wisdom, prices have already been pushed above their natural level.

- **We believe we're above average** (also called the 'Lake Wobegon Syndrome') – As we decide whether to join in with the latest savings fad, we don't see ourselves as lemmings running to financial loss along with hundreds of thousands of others. Instead, because we think that we are above average, we justify our actions by convincing ourselves that we have thought through the value of what we are about to buy and the reasons why we are making a good decision.

- **We're allergic to losing money** – If we have bought too high, at some point prices will peak and then fall. At first we tend to hold on in the hope that prices will rise again. But when this doesn't happen, we join the stampede towards the exit and sell in order to try to limit our losses.

- **We over-react** – Many of us tend to over-react to good and bad news. We become what are called 'noise investors'. With journalists desperate to grab our attention by sensationalising every little event in stock markets or property prices or the level of gold or the price of silver or interest rates, there's plenty of good and bad news (noise) almost every day to over-react to. But, by jumping around from one investment to another, we massively increase the costs we pay in fees and commissions and decimate any possible returns.

- **We make decisions on simplistic stimuli** – Most of us don't have the time or knowledge to do detailed analyses of every financial product we buy and so decide on very limited and usually misleading data. For example, we put money in the top-performing unit trust without realising that most top-performers gather so much money that they lose their flexibility and then have a series of dismal years. Or we're seduced by the guarantee offered by a stock-market bond or annuity without investigating how much we're actually being charged for the guarantee and whether we'd be better off without the hugely expensive guarantee.

- **We have 'home bias'** – If we're going to buy shares, unit trusts or property, we'll tend to put most of our money in companies or investments in our home country. This may make sense as that's what we know best, but it could mean we miss out on better opportunities.

If we really want to make money on our savings, we have to have the courage and emotional discipline to go against the crowd – to buy when everyone else is selling and sell when everyone is buying. Few of us can do this. Or if we're content with reasonable returns, we have to learn how to hold on for the longer term and not be spooked by short-term events and seemingly dramatic price moves. But if we're strongly influenced by what others are doing; or the thought of losing twenty to thirty per cent of our savings keeps us awake at night; or a rapid rise in the value of our investments convinces us that we're smarter than the person next door, then we run the risk of being one of the majority of people who make financial services insiders rich when we buy the wrong things too often at the wrong time and usually end up paying far too much and getting too little back.

Reason 10

We haven't made a financial plan

Lots of planners, but no plans

There are probably over a hundred thousand people in Britain who make an extremely comfortable living claiming to help us plan our finances. They go under different names – financial advisers, financial planners, pensions consultants, retirement planners, wealth managers and so on. However, one study of about ten thousand people who used financial planners found that not a single one of the ten thousand actually had anything remotely resembling a financial plan. Many financial planners and advisers aren't financial planners or advisers at all. They are just salespeople pushing a fairly limited range of financial products that earn them and their employer the highest level of income. Too often this means encouraging us to buy expensive, complex and risky products many of which will destroy rather than grow our wealth. The better financial planners might genuinely try to guide us towards what they believe are the most appropriate places to put our money to get the best return for the level of risk that we are prepared to take. However, deciding how to distribute our money between cash, bonds and shares or choosing some company's Global Growth Fund rather than another firm's Emerging Markets Income Fund is just making an investment choice, it is not real financial planning.

A proper financial plan means laying out a timeline for your life starting where you currently are and ending somewhere around the age of eighty five to ninety – or earlier if you're a bit of a pessimist and, of course, later if you're rather optimistic about your chances of remaining on this earth a little longer than most other people. On this timeline you need to put in how much you expect to earn each year and how much you think you'll spend, taking account of things like buying a home, educating your children, having a few holidays and so on. A critical part of your plan is the date you decide to reduce your working hours and/or retire. Your adult life should be split into two parts – about forty to forty five years accumulating money and then up to thirty years living off your assets and the paltry sums the state might be able to give you for your pension.

Perhaps one of the most important decisions you'll make in your plan will be the level of income you want to have once you've stopped work and so are no longer earning. When you know this, you can then calculate how much you need to accumulate throughout your working life. Given the continually falling level of annuity rates and the extraordinarily poor value offered by most annuity providers, you might get a shock when you realise just how much you're going to need to save during your working life. As I'll explain later, *Reason 36 – We hope that healthy savings will give us a healthy pension*, anyone with less than half a million pounds in savings, investments and pension funds in addition to their home is going to be slightly disappointed about the level of comfort in which they'll be able to spend their 'golden years' unless they're used to living extremely modestly and are happy being in an unheated home and using their tea bags two or three times.

Once you've laid out your timeline with your earnings and outgoings and decided what level of assets you'll need to build up for when you retire, then you can work out either by yourself or with the aid of a financial expert how you're going to get where you need to be. This helps you decide where you should be putting your money – property, cash, bonds, pension, unit trusts, commodities, fine wines, rare butterflies, moringa tree plantations or whatever. In this way, your financial plan should lead to you making your savings and investment plan (see Figure 1)

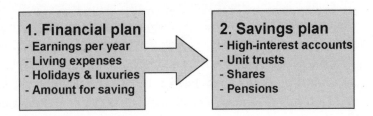

Figure 1 – We first need to do a real financial plan before we start choosing savings and investments

A crucial part of your savings and investment plan should be to do at least three scenarios so you can see what your life will be like if your assets give annual returns of say two, four and six per cent. Then each year you can monitor your actual progress to see what your savings are really achieving as this will give you a good idea of how many golfing trips and world cruises you'll be able to afford once you've opted for a life of retired leisure.

The huge majority of people in the financial services industry are only interested in getting our money, usually by making exaggerated promises either about the potential growth of the investments they're trying to flog us or about the supposedly rock-solid guarantees that we can't lose out by taking their supposed 'advice'. But all they're doing is trying to influence our savings and investment decisions, often to earn themselves the largest commissions. They are not giving us anything that in any way looks, smells or tastes like a financial plan. Laying out a real financial plan, as I've described above, is a useful and often sobering experience. I thoroughly recommend you try doing one. A first draft should only take you twenty to thirty minutes (see *Tip 2 – Make a Financial Plan*). Investing this time in your financial plan will help you make savings and investment decisions that are in your interest and not just in the interests of the financial salespeople and the multi-millionaire investment managers hoping to leech off considerable quantities of your hard-earned cash.

Reason 11

Banks love lazy and ignorant customers

However badly our banks treat us, most people's relationship with their bank will last much longer than their marriages. We're much more likely to get divorced than to change our bank. This customer inertia gives banks huge opportunities to profit from their customers as they know that few customers will bother with the administrative hassle of moving their business to a competitor. Moreover since the 2007 crash, several banks now own their former competitors, reducing our choice. So even if we did get in a huff over abysmal levels of service and move our money (or debts), we might well find that we are still with the same organisation even though we appear to be with a quite different bank.

Unfortunately, our loyalty to our banks costs us quite a lot of money - some studies have estimated that the average person who has placed their mortgage, current account, savings account and credit card with just one or at most two financial institutions is losing close to £3,000 a year from not buying the best products on the market in each category from different providers.[18]

Little interest in our interest

In Britain, we have about £59 billion in accounts paying no interest and another £313 billion in accounts with fairly laughable levels of interest. If we could just move about a third of this money to higher-interest accounts we'd be £2 billion to £3 billion a year – £8 million to £12 million a day – better off. Our banks would, of course, lose this £8 million to £12 million a day in profits were their customers to be a little more active in managing their money.

Some of us actually do take an interest in the interest rates we are getting and may have shifted our money to accounts where we genuinely believe we are receiving two or three per cent or more. However, in many cases we will have been tempted into apparently higher-interest accounts by introductory offers and bonuses. Typically such accounts might claim to pay interest of three per cent. But the bonus may account for over two per cent and the underlying interest may be less than one per cent. Once our money is safely in these accounts, the banks remove the bonuses, cutting the interest down to one per cent or less knowing that few customers will notice and even fewer will move their money. Even if the high interest we think we are getting doesn't include a bonus, banks are forever introducing new, fancy-sounding accounts while slashing the interest rates on their older, previously attractive accounts. On one account I held, I thought I was getting over four per cent. But when I rang my bank to check, I found this had actually been reduced over time to about 0.75 per cent.

Charges in through the back door

Not content with fleecing us by paying dismal to non-existent rates of interest, most banks have found another ingenious way of increasing the amount of money they earn from running our current accounts. The banks have always been nervous about the negative public relations fallout that would result from making us pay a fee for our current accounts. The present unpopularity of bankers makes introducing across-the-board fees pretty much impossible. However, as usual, banks have found a way round this potential problem. Rather than imposing current account fees on all of us, they have come up with the brilliant idea of convincing millions of us to pay for supposedly enhanced service. They have managed to sell us on the idea that we need to upgrade our current accounts to what they call 'packaged accounts' – accounts where we pay a monthly fee and also get things like travel insurance, car breakdown cover, commission-free travel money and various other flashing lights, bells and whistles. Many of us don't need these extras. We may even already have them from other sources. Others could buy these services much more cheaply elsewhere. But over five million of us have either agreed to taking packaged accounts or else have been automatically 'upgraded' without our knowledge from our free accounts to these expensive new monstrosities by our ever caring banks. We five million customers pay about £12 a month on average for packaged accounts, giving our banks an extra £720 million a year – £3 million a day – of our money.

Stealing our tax-free benefits

Towards the end of every tax year our banks indulge in a frenzy of marketing to get us to take advantage of the tax benefits of putting some of our savings into a Cash ISA – a savings account where the interest earned is exempt from tax. These selling efforts seem to have been quite successful as we now have over £160 billion in Cash ISAs. There are a few Cash ISAs which pay reasonable interest rates, but on many the rates paid are little short of scandalous.

"Cash ISAs have been turned into a systematic swindle. Sniffing an easy profit banks and building societies have, from day one, undermined and perverted what should have been a clean and simple product."[19]

On the day I'm writing this section, the average Cash ISA interest rate seems to be around two per cent, while ordinary (not ISA) longer-term savings accounts are paying about 3.7 per cent. Given that we have to hold our money in Cash ISAs for several years to get the tax benefits, it seems reasonable to compare the interest we get from Cash ISAs with longer-term savings accounts. If we're paying tax at twenty per cent, then a longer-term savings account with pre-tax interest of 3.7 per cent would be giving us an after-tax return of 2.96 per cent, considerably higher than the two per cent from a Cash ISA. Even if we were paying tax at forty per cent, a 3.7 per cent savings account would be returning 2.22 per cent – still slightly higher than a Cash ISA. However, for a fifty per cent taxpayer, a Cash ISA would be marginally better than a savings account.

Of course, with so many different accounts paying different levels of interest, you can find Cash ISAs which may give good value. But the majority of us will probably discover that our Cash ISAs are paying such low levels of interest that we'd be better off putting our money in an ordinary longer-term savings account and paying the tax. By paying low rates of interest on ISAs, the banks are effectively stealing the tax benefits we think we are getting, making their Cash ISAs worse than worthless to many savers.

Reason 12

We believe money can be created by financial innovation

Fooled again

Over the last few years, we ordinary savers have been persuaded to borrow money using ostensibly innovative new products like 120 per cent mortgages, self-certified mortgages, adjustable rate mortgages and home equity release plans and to put our savings into novel schemes such as precipice bonds, kick-out bonds, high-yield bonds, combination bonds and sometimes misleadingly-named 'guaranteed' stock-market investments. At the same time our banks and the people who should have been looking after our savings and pensions have thrown hundreds of billions of our money into supposedly 'exciting' new financial inventions like credit default swaps (CDSs) and collateralized debt obligations (CDOs).

> **"Most so-called financial innovations are just new ways to fleece customers or hide risk, and all major financial crises have been associated with some financial innovation."**[20]

There are several common features between the new, usually complex financial products that we savers and the major financial institutions managing our money have bought. The products were created with the sole purpose of making massive amounts of money for the people who created and then aggressively sold them; few people actually understood what they were buying; and all the subsequent losses landed on the shoulders of ordinary people who saw their savings evaporate, their pension funds collapse in value, their homes repossessed, their jobs disappear and their taxes expropriated to both bail out the 'too-big-to-fail' financial institutions and also provide the avaricious but incompetent bosses of the financial institutions with many tens of billions in bonuses in spite of the fact that they wrecked the world's financial system.

Money from nothing

There have been many very beneficial financial innovations which have played an important role in supporting economic growth and wealth creation. The emergence of the Lloyds insurance market encouraged international trade; the development of limited liability companies fuelled investment in the industrial revolution; and in the high-tech boom venture capitalists provided much of the money to support technology companies which couldn't get funding from more traditional sources. Similarly, retail services like mortgage lending, ATMs, credit cards and unit trusts have enabled us to buy our own homes, helped generate consumer demand and allowed ordinary people to invest their savings to get some of the benefits of economic growth without the risks of having to buy individual shares themselves.

However, there have been many financial innovations which have served little or no productive purpose. Instead they have been largely created and promoted for what economists call 'rent seeking' – to make extraordinary profits for those who developed and ruthlessly sold them without creating value for the economy as a whole. Too many supposedly innovative financial products aimed at both big institutional investors and ordinary people have been complex, opaque, expensive and enormously destructive for those who bought them. For major investors we've had junk bonds in the 1970s which allowed one key trader to be paid over $700 million in just one of several very profitable years but lost billions for many of those who put their money in them. Then there were interest rate swaps in the 1980s providing eye-watering profits for the few at the expense of the many. The most recent example of financial innovations losing all touch with the real economy can be seen in the massive growth in the two products that have caused much of the 2007 to 2011 financial mayhem – CDOs repacking and selling mortgages and CDSs insurance policies taken out against risky loans. CDSs, for example, shot up from around $8 trillion in 2004 to $60 trillion by 2007 far outstripping the much more modest real growth in the GDPs of the US or the EU (see Figure 1).

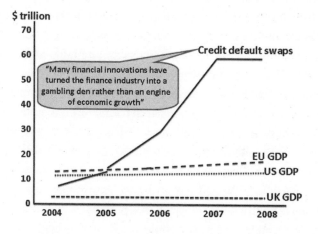

Figure 1 – The growth in Credit Default Swaps had nothing to do with real economic growth and everything to do with gambling

CDOs and CDSs were theoretically about spreading risk. Instead they just became a way for financial institutions to gamble with other people's money. As with all gambling, the casino owners - the product providers and salespeople - became unimaginably rich and ordinary people were mulcted.

For us ordinary savers there have been quite a few products that have made the originators and sellers richer while leaving many of us considerably poorer – mis-sold personal pensions, endowment mortgages, high income bonds, guaranteed investments, with-profits savings schemes, funds of funds for instance (see *Reason 1 – The financial jungle is a dangerous place*).

What you don't know can hurt you

The reason why financial innovations sell so well in spite of their long history of destroying the wealth of those who buy them is largely due to what experts call 'information asymmetry'. Basically, the people who design and sell new financial products know an awful lot more about them than the people buying them, just as a used car salesman has much more information about the real (usually appalling) condition of the wreck he is trying to flog you than you do. Information asymmetry puts the seller at a huge advantage over the buyer. The release of several embarrassing emails has indicated that the packagers of mortgages into CDOs were probably well aware that they had taken financial detritus, given it a lick of cheap paint and a quick polish and then had a compliant rating agency declare it was monetary magic. Only once they had bought this trash did many of the institutions to whom we entrusted our savings - banks, pension funds and life insurance companies – realise they'd been sold a very evil-smelling pig in a poke.

Similarly, most ordinary people faced with a bank or financial adviser promising guaranteed stock-market returns or kick-out bonds paying eight per cent a year or some other complicated product don't have sufficient knowledge to assess whether they're being sold gold-dust or garbage. Usually it's the latter for the buyer and the former for the seller.

The bottom line is that your savings can earn money either by lending them to a bank (deposit account), to a government (government bonds) or to a company (corporate bonds). Or else you can own part of a business by setting up your own company or by buying shares in someone else's in the hope that they'll make some profits and be generous enough to pay some of these to you each year in the form of dividends rather than putting them in their own pockets. But any new product which makes the process of investing or borrowing more complex, expensive or opaque has probably been designed in the interests of the seller rather than the buyer. It's often difficult for us to resist the blandishments of an over-eager salesperson, usually disguised as a financial consultant or retirement adviser or wealth manager, spouting endless enticing facts and figures as they try to tie us into some wonderful new saving, investing or borrowing scheme their masters have ordered them to sell. Similarly, when faced by an ace, jet-setting sales team from banks like Goldman Sachs or JP Morgan, unfortunately too few investment managers seem to have had either the wit or guile to see through whatever over-priced rubbish was being foisted upon them. But we, and the massive financial institutions that should be safeguarding our money, need to be wary of anyone who seems unnaturally enthusiastic about making money for us with their latest financial invention. Too often only one side will make money from the deal and it's seldom the buyer.

Reason 13

We fall for the "Money Illusion"

The Money Illusion is a term generally attributed to economist John Maynard Keynes. It describes our tendency to think of money in nominal terms – its numerical/face value – rather than in real terms – its actual purchasing power. This leads us to make poor decisions as we tend not to fully account for the relentless way inflation erodes the value of our money. For example, numerous studies have shown that someone getting a five per cent pay rise when inflation is at four per cent feels happier than a person given a two per cent pay rise when there is no inflation, even though the latter is logically better off. Similarly, a person whose pay is cut by two per cent at a time of no inflation experiences a greater sense of injustice than someone who is given a one per cent pay increase when inflation is four per cent, despite the fact that the former is actually better off.

Although first proposed in the early twentieth century, the prevalence of the Money Illusion has been confirmed more recently by tests using MRI scanning. These showed that the part of the brain associated with responding to anticipated or received rewards was more active giving people greater pleasure and satisfaction the higher the nominal amount received, even if it had a lower real value. We have a tendency to react to numbers without trying to understand what the numbers really mean. In a way this is similar to how we respond to prices. We all understand that there is no real difference between say a DVD costing £9.99 and one priced at £10.00 or a car being sold at £9,990 rather than at £10,000. But as shops and car dealers around the world know, we still have the impression that the items at £9.99 and £9,990 are somehow much better value than things priced a tiny 0.1 per cent higher.

The Money Illusion affects our savings and pensions choices in two main ways. In times of low inflation, we underestimate the real returns we are getting on our savings causing us to make rash and risky decisions with our money. When inflation is higher, we fail to realise the corrosive effects that inflation will have on our savings and retirement income and find we have not accumulated enough to give us the lifestyle we had originally planned for.

Rushing where the grass seems greener

For the last few years until governments started trying to inflate their way out of debt in 2010, inflation rates in developed countries were running at historically low levels of two to two and a half per cent. The rates savers were receiving on their cash savings were also low – from 2006 to 2010 you could get four to five per cent in a two- to three-year deposit account. The press was full of stories about how returns for savers had fallen to derisory levels and millions were encouraged by banks, financial advisers and personal finance journalists to abandon the relative safety of their deposit accounts and instead put their money into bonds and investments linked to stock markets. Sure enough, ordinary people withdrew tens of billions from deposit accounts and poured them into riskier investments and in the process lost several billion to finance professionals by paying them commissions, fees, management charges, purchasing costs, dealing charges and other expenses. The problem is that many savers may have been reacting to the Money Illusion rather than to any actual decline in the real returns they were getting from their bank deposit accounts.

If we take a straightforward example, the long-term return on cash held in a bank has been around is 2.3 per cent. Let's say that at a time of low inflation of two per cent, a person is being paid interest of 4.3 per cent. A few years earlier that person might have been getting 7.3 per cent when inflation was up around five per cent. Let's assume that person had £40,000 in savings – this was quite a common figure for many people encouraged by their banks to move from deposit accounts to very risky investment bonds. Assuming the person was paying twenty per cent tax, at a time of low inflation they would have been getting real returns of £576 a year after tax and inflation. But when inflation was high they were only receiving £336 after tax and inflation (see Figure 1).

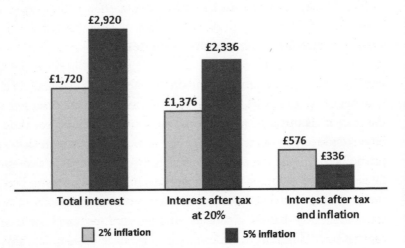

Figure 1 – The Money Illusion makes people feel they are getting better returns when interest rates and inflation are higher although they are actually getting less (returns on £40,000 savings at 2% and 5% inflation).

So although they felt they were getting more money when interest rates were 7.3 per cent and inflation was high, after tax and inflation are taken into account they were better off with low interest rates and low inflation. The problem here is that we are taxed on the nominal interest we receive rather than the real interest. So we are paying tax on inflation. The higher inflation is, the more tax we pay and so the lower our real returns are. Yet many millions felt better off receiving 7.3 per cent at a time of higher inflation rather than 4.3 per cent when inflation was lower. They fell for the Money Illusion.

Clearly, if the person was not paying tax, the real returns with both low and higher inflation are the same 2.3 per cent. However, if the person was paying tax at thirty or even forty per cent, then the difference between the low inflation and high inflation is even more marked with the person earning £232 a year after tax at forty per cent and inflation when inflation was low, but losing £248 a year when inflation was higher.

The Money Illusion may be partly to blame for a stampede of savers from bank deposit accounts into investments like bonds and shares in search of higher returns. But most of those involved in the stampede will probably lose money. Firstly, all of them will have sacrificed up to three per cent of their money in fees, charges and a wide range of other costs. Secondly, the flood of money pushed up the price of bonds and shares so that many of the stampeders were buying at inflated prices. Thirdly, most of those who bought bonds probably haven't understood that by late 2011 or early 2012, interest rates are likely to have started to go up again. As interest rates rise, the price of fixed-interest bonds always falls. So when the stampeders eventually sell their bonds, they will probably make a capital loss. As for those who bought shares, they seem to have inflated stock markets above their average long-term values at a time when companies' ability to earn profits is going to be constrained by the need for governments to reduce their deficits and debts by cutting public spending and raising taxes. It's impossible to predict where stock markets will be in two or three years time, but there are strong indications that they are currently slightly overvalued (see *Reason 18 – We think stock markets will always rise*). So it does seem as if many of those people who fell for the Money Illusion and rushed out of safe bank deposit accounts when interest rates and inflation were low may end up worse off than if they had left their money where it was. But financial industry insiders will make fortunes from the rush of money from one place to another caused by people deceived by the Money Illusion

How to halve the value of your money

During our working lives most of us probably don't worry too much about inflation – partly because wages usually rise above or at least in line with inflation and partly because the more experienced we are in our careers, the higher our earnings are likely to be and so the more likely they are to outstrip inflation. Moreover, if we've taken out a mortgage to buy a home, a healthy rate of inflation can seem to cut our monthly repayments making them more manageable and giving us more spending money. However for the retired, after ill health inflation is probably is probably the greatest threat to their retirement wellbeing. Unless they have an inflation-protected pension, inflation will probably halve their real earnings and maybe even cut them by three quarters between the day they retire and the time they shuffle unsteadily or are pushed by a hospital-acquired infection off this mortal coil.

Real spending power of £20,000 a year		
Annual inflation		
Age	2%	4%	6%
65	£20,000	£20,000	£20,000
70	£18,000	£16,300	£14,700
75	£16,300	£13,300	£10,800
80	£14,800	£10,800	£7,900
85	£13,300	£8,800	£5,800
90	£12,000	£7,200	£4,300
95	£11,000	£5,900	£3,100

Figure 2 – Even low levels of inflation can slash a pensioner's real spending power

Over the last half century inflation has averaged just over six per cent a year. At six per cent a year, someone retiring at sixty five would have seen their spending power halve by the time they reach seventy five and drop to around a quarter if they live to eighty five (see Figure 2).

With current life expectancy for retirees at over eighty five years, if inflation continues to run at its historic average, then anyone retiring on a fixed income will see the real value of their money fall by three quarters before they die. Even if inflation hovers between two and four per cent, most pensioners will see a drastic reduction in their spending power. That's something to worry about if you think your parents or you might need to pay nursing home fees of up to £30,000 a year for their or your final years.

Reason 14

There will always be bubbles

Forever blowing bubbles

Understanding financial bubbles is important because at some point in our savings lives most of us will lose money as the result of one or several bubbles. We all probably know about the greatest financial bubbles in history – Dutch tulips in the 1630s, the South Sea Bubble in 1711-1720, the Roaring Twenties stock market bubble which led to the Wall Street Crash in 1929, Japanese property in the 1980s, the high tech bubble in the late 1990s and the property bubble and crash of the last few years. But there have been many other major bubbles – canals in Britain in the 1830s, railroads in the US and Europe in the 1850s and Florida building in the 1920s. As we look back, we probably wonder why so many people were foolish enough to be caught up in previous financial bubbles. Yet in recent years, in spite of all the analysis and investment research done by tens of thousands of financial experts, we've possibly had more bubbles than at any time in history. In addition to the dotcom and the subprime mortgage boom-and-busts, there have been bubbles in buy-to-let properties, gold, uranium, Eastern European holiday homes, Spanish properties, timeshares, commodities, oil prices, emerging markets, jojoba beans and even exotic livestock production – llamas, wild boar and ostriches amongst others.

Each of us will probably live through at least two major bubbles and maybe five to ten smaller ones. Even if our money doesn't go directly into a bubble through our own savings or pension funds, we can suffer indirectly as bursting bubbles tend to damage economic growth and so impact all of us.

Here we go again

Most bubbles tend to follow a very similar pattern and go through about six stages (see Figure 1)

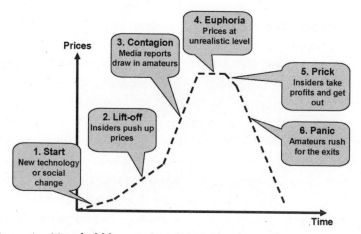

Figure 1 – Most bubbles consist of six main phases

1. **Start** – The majority of bubbles begin as a result of a genuine technical breakthrough like canals, railways, the telegraph or the Internet or a social change like the baby boom generation having large amounts of disposable income to buy shares, unit trusts, buy-to-let properties or holiday homes.

2. **Lift-off** – Bubbles tend to begin gradually as those in the know realise there is a new opportunity and are the first movers into whatever is going on.

3. **Contagion** – The media picks up the story and there are endless articles by journalists sensationalising what is

happening and gushing about the enormous profits to be made. Those with a vested interest eagerly promote the benefits of whatever's 'hot' and many thousands of us believe them. Ordinary people start to feel that they're missing something and don't want to be left out. They jump in and prices start to shoot up. For example, believe it or not we were once told, 'The ostrich industry is the fastest growing agricultural business in the world. With the vast array and almost unlimited supply of products and services that we have available, your opportunities to resell these products has never been better' (see Figure 2).

Figure 2 – In the ostrich-farming bubble, thousands of people thought this chap was worth over £10,000

4. **Euphoria** – As ever more amateurs cast caution aside and rush to join the parade, it seems that nobody can lose. Values reach levels that defy all logic – property in Tokyo once cost over three hundred times what it cost in New York or London; dotcom companies which never made a profit became worth hundreds of millions with some even topping a billion; you could sell an ostrich (not the most beautiful, friendly or tasty of birds) for over ten thousand pounds, dollars or euros.

5. **Prick** – Insiders realise that prices are unsustainable and bail out making massive profits as they sell their holdings

to the worst suckers – the Johnny-come-latelies.

6. **Panic** – Prices wobble and then start to fall. People get nervous and try to sell. But there aren't enough buyers and prices plummet ever faster in a self-reinforcing downward spiral as more and more investors rush for the exits. Journalists and other experts suddenly get 20/20 vision in hindsight and the media is full of stories about how whatever was in fashion was actually overpriced and so the crash was inevitable.

Why bubbles happen

Although there have always been bubbles, experts have had difficulty explaining why they happen, especially nowadays when we have huge numbers of financial analysts and researchers across the world with vast amounts of computing power repeatedly analysing every company, commodity and property to establish their precise value. Moreover, we have the Internet allowing users access to more information than has ever been available before.

One cause of bubbles seems to be low interest rates. When interest rates fall below a certain level, a tsunami of cash pours out of savings into shares, property, gold, ostriches, moringa trees or whatever in search of higher returns. Once some of the money goes into the latest thing, prices start to rise attracting even more money, pushing prices further upwards. This draws in yet more money and so on till prices shoot up, stall and then crash. Another explanation is our tendency towards 'herd behaviour' – if everyone else is piling into something, we feel that others may know something we don't and so we should be in there too. Later, when it goes horribly wrong, we can justify to ourselves that we made the right decision at the time because we were only doing what other reasonably intelligent people were also doing.

One reason bubbles burst is that the early movers realise prices are unsustainably high and so cash in walking away with huge profits. But another cause of bursting bubbles is that there is too much money chasing too few good assets, so a lot of the money ends up bloating the price of assets that cannot give decent returns. For example, the first canals, railway lines, dotcom companies or buy-to-let properties were probably great investments. But as more canals or railways were built and as more dotcom companies or buy-to-let properties came onto the market, the market became saturated, the Law of Diminishing Returns kicked in, nobody could make decent profits and prices collapsed.

Although bubbles harm many ordinary people who lose money and can slow economic growth in the short term, they can actually contribute to a country's longer-term economic success. The flood of money into successive bubbles may have led to a series of spectacular financial booms and busts, but they also fed massive investment in telegraph, railways, canals and broadband networks which eventually were essential foundations for subsequent economic expansion.

Who gets hurt?

The first movers into and out of a bubble will make fortunes. After the 2007 stock-market crash, I interviewed a banker and asked him if he and his colleagues lost money from their investments falling in value. He laughed and said, 'of course not, we could see it coming and got out before all the suckers realised what was about to happen'. Insiders in any market – shares, properties, gold, ostriches – will spend eight to ten hours a day working in, thinking about and discussing that market with other insiders. They will detect exactly what is going on and be able to protect their assets and make huge profits by getting in and out in time. However, most ordinary people might read the occasional newspaper article or see a TV report and so will not realise there's a party until it's well under way and will not know that the party is over until it's far too late.

"If your taxi driver tells you to buy gold, then it's time to sell."[21]

There seem to be three main groups hurt by each bubble. The largest is ordinary people suckered into betting their money by the torrent of stories about how easy profits can be made quickly. Pension funds also get caught in the larger financial bubbles. Because they often have cautious investment policies, they tend to get into expanding markets late when prices are already high and then bail out late when prices have fallen as they desperately try to protect what is left of their assets. There have also been studies which have shown that younger unit trust investment managers perform worse during bubbles than older ones who might have already lived through one or more bubbles and so don't get swept up by the irrational enthusiasm.

The next bubble

At the time of writing, with bank interest rates depressingly low a large amount of money seems to be sloshing around the world in search of a home. It appears that there are several bubbles rapidly inflating in things like gold prices, green energy, corporate bonds and Chinese shares, to name a few. No doubt there are others which are not yet clear. But the moral of the story is that unless you are absolutely sure that you are getting in at the early stages of a bubble; are confident that you know when to bail out; and have the emotional discipline to get out when you've made a good profit rather than hanging on too long in the hope of making even more money, then you should steer clear of bubbles. A recent article was titled *Riding The Market Bubble: Don't Try This At Home.*[22]

That seems like pretty good advice.

Reason 15

Moving money is bad for our wealth

The Laws of Financial Physics

Although there are few certainties in the world of savings and investments, there are some things which are completely predictable. One is, of course, that the people handling our money will always have bigger houses, better holidays and flashier cars than we do. Another immutable law is what we could call the 'Law of Profitable Motion' – the more our money moves, the more of it will disappear into other people's pockets making them wealthier and us poorer in the process. Bank advisers, financial advisers, personal finance journalists, unit trust salespeople, pension planners, retirement counsellors and a host of others are endlessly exhorting us to keep moving our money from one investment to another supposedly to get benefits like better returns or guarantees or security or regular growth or improved service or whatever. But usually their advice is tainted by the fact that each time we listen to them, they get a slice of our money either directly in the form of fees and commissions or indirectly as when journalists get junkets, investment tips or other favours from financial services firms whose products they puff.

There are two main ways that moving our money makes other people rich – up-front fees and churning.

Paying at the door

With unit trusts, most of us probably realise that we are paying about five per cent up-front to buy into whatever unit trust we have chosen or has been recommended to us. But with other products like investment plans, guaranteed bonds, combination bonds, pensions and life assurance, few people will ever find out what they are actually being charged when they sign up. Typical fees charged by banks selling an investment product are around three to three and a half per cent. In the last couple of years, as interest rates have remained low, many pensioners with six-figure savings were encouraged by their banks to potentially get higher income by switching their money from relatively safe bank and building society deposit accounts into five- or six-year investment plans. Just half and hour's work setting up a scheme moving say £200,000 of a pensioner's life savings into such a product could earn the bank £6,000 to £7,000 which would, of course, be cut directly from that customer's savings.

With a life insurance policy, the salesperson may be getting close to ten percent of the first year's payments. As about a third of people abandon their life insurance policies within five years of starting them, many of us end up paying for absolutely nothing at all while the salespeople and the insurance companies make a comfortable living.

An adviser selling and setting up a company pension scheme could be skimming off anywhere from twenty to seventy per cent of each employee's first-year or first two years' contributions in addition to an ongoing commission of a half to one per cent. So, even a tiny scheme with just a thousand employees paying in £3,000 a year each in employer and employee contributions could easily earn the administrator £2 million to £4 million for organising the scheme and £15,000 or more a year for acting as an occasional go-between between the employer and the pensions firm. Setting up a larger scheme for ten thousand or more contributors would be just like printing money.

Churning – faster, faster!

The financial services industry seems to have been hugely accelerating the rate at which it has been moving our money and thus the amount it creams off for itself. In the early 1970s, the average investor on the New York Stock Exchange held their shares for around five years, now it's less than a year. But jumping in and out of investments is a mug's game – the only sure winners are the middlemen who take a cut of our money each time it moves. This acceleration in the movement of our money partly reflects that fact that the big institutions like unit trusts and pension funds, which manage our money, are turning over their portfolios much faster and also that individual investors are buying and selling their shares much more frequently than in the past.

Unit trusts are probably the most common way for ordinary people to put their savings in shares. In 2007 the turnover – the proportion of shares held by unit trusts that were sold and bought each year – was around thirty per cent, meaning that investments were being held for about three years. By 2010 turnover had increased to over eighty per cent because unit trusts were only holding shares for around fifteen months. This increase in turnover over the last few years has probably added at least one per cent to the costs paid by investors. With over £500 billion held by British savers in unit trusts, the increase in turnover rates possibly extracts over £5 billion a year more from savers – about £20 million each working day – and thus makes financial industry insiders £20 million a day wealthier at our expense. If, as is likely, there has been a similar increase in turnover rates of the £800 billion held in pension funds, then that's another £8 billion a year more taken from us ordinary savers – £30 million or so a day – and given to the people managing our money.

We've become speculators, not investors

Many more experienced investors emphasise the difference between investing and speculating. Buying a company's shares or a buy-to-let property and holding them for several years to benefit from both income and capital growth can be considered as investing. Buying and selling shares every few months or jumping from one unit trust to another every couple of years is either intentional speculation or just blind chasing after returns. Unless you are a financial services insider with access to privileged information, neither speculation nor panicked rushing from one thing to the next is going to make you rich.

"Only one thing eats up investment returns faster than fees and commissions, and that is frequent trading. Do not succumb."[23]

The longer you hold an investment, the greater your chance of making a positive return, unless there is a major crash just before you decide to sell. The more you speculate, the more of your money you hand over to financial services insiders. With investing, we're relying on the underlying value of the assets we buy to provide income and growth, with speculating we're betting that we can predict short-term movements in prices caused by immediate economic developments or anticipate the herd behaviour of other savers and gamblers. There are people who do become extraordinarily wealthy from speculation. Some are excellent analysts and others are brilliant psychologists and so they can make fortunes outguessing their less gifted competitors. Many other market insiders take a more direct route to making their fortunes and rely on insider trading or share price manipulation to amass their millions (see *Reason 23 – Stock markets may be rigged against us*). But for the majority of us, speculation is unlikely to make us wealthier, but it will transfer a lot of our money into someone else's pockets.

The arrival of the Internet and fast broadband has given ordinary savers direct access to financial markets around the world and the ability to actively trade in tens of thousands of shares, commodities, contracts for difference, futures, foreign exchange and other financial products. The benefit of this is that it has pulled transaction costs down by decreasing the role of middlemen and allowing more companies to compete for our business. But the drawback is that instant-access, low-cost trading has encouraged something resembling hyperactivity amongst some savers. The ultimate consequence of this has been to enable many ordinary people to try their hands at day trading, which transforms speculation into something resembling a video game.

"For the typical retail investor, day trading isn't investing, it's gambling. If you want to gamble, go to Las Vegas; the food is better."[24]

Day traders buy or sell shares, commodities, currencies or other financial products within one trading day. Sometimes they may only hold what they buy for a few seconds. In theory, day trading shouldn't be too difficult. For very little expense you can buy software which will spot when the price of any share, commodity, currency or whatever has begun to move either upwards or downwards. The trader can then try to jump in and out quickly to profit from the movement. But studies have shown that most day traders lose money most of the time. About nine out of ten new traders lose all their capital and give up within their first year. However, the survivors do much better with around half of them making money regularly over a period of several years. One to two per cent of day traders will make millions.

For most of us, when we or the firms which manage our savings endlessly move our money, we're being lured into playing a fool's game. But it's a game that advisers, salespeople, banks and personal finance journalists increasingly encourage us to play as it makes them rich at our expense. It's difficult not to be tempted by stories of the profits to be made by getting into the next savings and investment 'big thing'. But those who resist the temptation to play the money-moving game will usually find themselves better off than those who rush around forever chasing the mirage of higher returns.

Reason 16

Financial advisers may be acting in their own interests

Heroes or villains?

"All industries have a few bad apples. I would say that 80% of financial advisers are either good or very good"[25]

or

"It's just 99% of financial advisers who give the rest of us a bad name"

Financial advisers, also called financial consultants, financial planners, retirement planners or wealth advisers, occupy a strange position amongst the ranks of those who would sell to us. With most other sellers, whether they are pushing cars, clothes, condos or condoms, we understand that they're just doing a job and we accept that the more they sell to us, the more they should earn. But the proposition that financial advisers come with is unique. They claim, or at least intimate, that they can make our money grow by more than if we just shoved it into a long-term, high-interest bank account. If they couldn't suggest they could find higher returns than a bank account, then there would be no point in us using them. Yet, if they really possessed the mysterious alchemy of getting money to grow, why would they tell us? Why wouldn't they just keep their secrets to themselves in order to make themselves rich?

The answer, of course, is that most financial advisers are not expert horticulturalists able to grow money nor are they alchemists who can transform our savings into gold. The only way they can earn a crust is by taking a bit of everything we, their clients, save. Sadly for us, most financial advisers are just salespeople whose standard of living depends on how much of our money they can encourage us to put through their not always caring hands. And whatever portion of our money they take for themselves to pay for things like their mortgages, pensions, cars, holidays, golf club fees, restaurant meals and children's education must inevitably make us poorer.

To make a reasonable living, a financial adviser will probably have costs of about £100,000 to £200,000 a year in salary, office expenses, secretarial support, travel costs, marketing, communications and other bits and pieces. So a financial adviser has to take in between £2,000 and £4,000 a week in fees and commissions, either as an employee or running their own business. I'm guessing that on average financial advisers will have between fifty and eighty clients. Of course, some successful ones will have many more and those who are struggling will have fewer. This means that each client will be losing somewhere between £1,250 and £4,000 a year from their investments and pension savings either directly in upfront fees or else indirectly in commissions paid to the adviser by financial products suppliers. All the fee-based advisers I've spoken to have a minimum charge of £3,000 a year with several looking for about £5,000 before they would consider it worth their while helping me manage my financial affairs. Advisers would probably claim that their specialist knowledge more than compensates for the amounts they squirrel away for themsleves in commissions and fees. But numerous studies around the world, decades of financial products mis-selling scandals and the disappointing returns on many of our investments and pensions savings should serve as an almost deafening warning to any of us tempted to entrust our own and our family's financial futures to someone trying to make a living by offering us financial advice.

Who gets rich – clients or advisers?

There are six main ways that financial advisers get paid:

Pay-Per Trade – The adviser takes a flat fee or a percentage fee every time the client buys, sells or invests. Most stockbrokers use this approach.

Fee only – There are a very small number of financial advisers (it varies from around five to ten percent in different countries) who charge an hourly fee for all the time they use advising us and helping to manage our money.

Commission-based – The large majority of advisers get paid mainly from commissions by the companies whose products they sell to us.

Fee-based – Over the years there has been quite a lot of concern about commission-based advisers pushing clients' money into savings schemes which pay the biggest commissions and so are wonderful for advisers but may not give the best returns for savers. To overcome clients' possible mistrust of their motives in making investment recommendations, many advisers now claim to be 'fee-based'. However, some critics have called this a 'finessing' of the reality that they still make most of their money from commissions even if they do charge an often reduced hourly fee for their services.

Free! – If your bank finds out that you have money to invest, they will quickly usher you into the office of their in-house financial adviser. Here you will apparently get expert advice about where to put your money completely free of charge. But usually the bank is only offering a limited range of products from just a few financial services companies and the bank's adviser is a commission-based salesperson. With both the bank and the adviser taking a cut for every product sold to you, that inevitably reduces your savings.

Performance-related – There are a few advisers who will accept to work for somewhere between ten and twenty per cent of the annual profits made on their clients' investments. This is usually only available to wealthier clients with investment portfolios of over a million pounds.

Each of these payment methods has advantages and disadvantages for us. With **pay-per-trade** we know exactly how much we will pay and we can decide how many or few trades we wish to do. The problem is, of course, that it is in the adviser's interest that we make as many trades as possible and there may be an almost irresistible temptation for pay-per-trade advisers to encourage us to churn our investments – constantly buying and selling - so they can make money, rather than advising us to leave our money for several years in particular shares, unit trusts or other financial products.

Fee-only advisers usually charge about the same as a lawyer or surveyor – in the range of £100 to £200 an hour, though many will have a minimum fee of about £3,000 a year. As with pay-per-trade, the investor should know exactly how much they will be paying. But anyone who has ever dealt with fee-based businesses – lawyers, accountants, surveyors, architects, management consultants, computer repair technicians and even car mechanics – will know that the amount of work supposedly done (and thus the size of the fee) will often inexplicably expand to what the fee-earner thinks can be reasonably extracted from the client almost regardless of the amount of real work actually needed or done.

The commission paid to **commission-based** advisers is generally split into two parts. The 'upfront commission' is paid by the financial product manufacturers to the advisers as soon as we invest, then every year after that the adviser will get a 'trailing commission'. Upfront commissions on stock-market funds can range from three to four per cent, with trailing commissions of up to one per cent. On pension funds, the adviser could get anywhere from twenty to seventy five per cent of our first year's or two years' payments in upfront commission. Over the longer term, the trailing commission will fall to about a half a per cent. There are some pension plans which pay less in upfront commission. But for reasons which should need no explanation, these tend to be less popular with too many financial advisers. With commission-based advisers there are several risks for investors. The first is what's called 'commission bias' – that advisers will extol the massive potential returns for us on those products which earn them the most money. So they will tend to encourage us to put our money into things like unit trusts, funds of funds, investment bonds and offshore tax-reduction wrappers – all products which pay generous commissions. They are less likely to mention things like index-tracker unit trusts and exchange traded funds as these pay little or no commissions but may be much better for our financial health. Moreover, by setting different commission levels on different products, it's effectively the manufacturers who decide which products financial advisers energetically push and which they hold back on. Secondly, the huge difference between upfront and trailing commissions means that it's massively in the advisers' interest to keep our money moving into new investments. One very popular trick at the moment is for advisers to contact people who have been saving for many years into a pension fund and suggest we move our money. Pension fund management fees have dropped over the last ten to twenty years, so it's easy for the adviser to sit a client down, show us the figures and convince us to transfer our pension savings to one of the newer, lower-cost pension products. When doing this, advisers can immediately pocket anywhere from three to over seven per cent of our total pension savings, yet most of us could complete the necessary paperwork ourselves in less than twenty minutes.

As many **fee-based** advisers actually earn most of their money from commissions, like commission-based advisers they can easily fall victim to commission bias when trying to decide which investments to propose to us.

Most of us will meet a bank's apparently **'free'** in-house adviser if we have a reasonable amount of money in our current account or if we ask about depositing our savings in a longer-term, higher interest account. Typically we'll be encouraged by the front-desk staff to take a no-cost meeting with a supposed 'finance and investment specialist'. Their job will be to first point out the excellent and competitively high interest rates offered by the bank, which are in fact rarely either high or competitive. But then they will tell us that we're likely to get even better returns if we put our money into one of the investment products that they recommend. We will be given a choice of investment options and risk profiles. However, the bank will earn much more from us from the manufacturer's commission selling us a product which is not guaranteed to return all our capital, than it would if we just chose to put our money in a virtually risk-free deposit account. A £50,000 investment, for example, could give the bank an immediate £1,500 to £2,000 (depending on the commission rate) in upfront commission plus another £250 to £500 each year in trailing commission – easy money for little effort.

Should you have over one million pounds, euros or dollars to invest, you might find an adviser willing to be **paid according to the performance** of your investments. One problem is that the adviser will be happy to share the pleasure of your profits in good years, but they'll be reluctant to join you in the pain of your losses when times are tough. So, most will offer to take a hefty fee when the value of your investments rises and a reduced fee if you lose money. Yet they will generally not ever take a hit however much your investments go down in value. The benefit with performance pay for advisers is that they will be motivated to maximise your returns in order to maximise their earnings. The worry might be that they could take excessive risks, comfortable in the knowledge that even if you make a loss they'll still get a basic fee.

In theory, by 2012 all Britain's advisers should be moving away from commissions and only charging fees which should be clearly explained to their customers. But experience suggests that those in the financial services industry have an awfully long history of repeatedly finding creative ways of getting around the few restrictions our half-hearted regulators have tried to impose on them. So anyone hoping that the financial advice business will suddenly become totally open and honest within our lifetimes might end up being more than disappointed.

Am I qualified? I've written a book!

One worrying feature with financial advisers is that it doesn't seem to be terribly difficult to set yourself up as one. Of about 250,000 registered financial advisers in the USA, only about 56,500 have the most commonly-recognised qualification. Some of the others have other diplomas and awards, but the large majority don't. One source suggested that there may be as many as 165,000 people in Britain calling themselves financial advisers.[26] Of these about 28,000 are registered with the Financial Services Authority as independent financial advisers and will have some qualifications, often a diploma. It's not clear how many of the others are suitably qualified to offer financial advice. The in-house financial advisers in banks will usually just have been through a few one-day or half-day internal training courses in how to sell the particular products that the bank wants to sell. So they will know a bit about the products recommended by that bank and the main arguments to convince us that putting our money into them is much more sensible than sticking it in a high-interest account. But they will probably not know much about anything else. Or, even if they are knowledgeable, they won't give us any objective advice as they'll have strict sales targets to meet to get their bonuses and promotion.

However in the world of financial advisers, not having any real qualifications is not the same as not having any real qualifications. There are quite a few training firms springing up which offer financial advisers two- to three-day training courses which will give attendees an impressive-looking diploma. Or if they can't be bothered doing the course, advisers can just buy bogus financial-adviser qualifications on the Internet. A few of these on an office wall can do much to reassure a nervous investor that their money will be in safe and experienced hands. Moreover, financial advisers can also pay specialist marketing support companies to provide them with printed versions of learned articles about investing with the financial adviser's name and photo on them as ostensibly being the author. A further scam, seen in the USA but probably not yet spread to other countries, is for a financial adviser to pay to have themselves featured as the supposed author of a book about investing, which can be given out to potential clients to demonstrate the adviser's credentials. If we're impressed by a few certificates on a wall, then we're likely to be doubly so by apparently published articles and books. In one investigation, journalists found copies of the same book about safe investing for senior citizens ostensibly written by four quite different and unrelated advisers, each of whom would have paid several thousand dollars for the privilege of getting copies of the book they had not written with themselves featured as the author.

Of course, only a very small number of financial advisers would resort to tricks like fake qualifications, false articles and bogus books. But the main point here is that far too many of them may know a lot about a few specific products which they are highly incentivised to sell, but may be insufficiently qualified to offer us genuine financial advice suited to our particular circumstances.

Reason 17

We mess up when using a financial adviser

With hundreds of different kinds of bank account, pension plans, life insurance products and annuities on the market and over six thousand unit trusts offered by hundreds of fund management companies, it's understandable that many of us feel we have neither the time nor the expertise to choose which is best for us. So we decide to put our financial fate in the hands of one of Britain's many thousands of genuine or self-styled financial advisers. We might be lucky and find an adviser who is both knowledgeable about the market and also working in our best interests, rather than one pushing a narrow range of products that earn them the highest commission rates. Financial advisers are not all bad and some will genuinely try to help us make the best decisions, but many of us lose money by making stupid mistakes in the way we use our advisers.

Mistake 1 – We expect our adviser to 'beat the market'

One of the big selling points advisers often use to convince us to use their services is that they can get us higher returns on our savings and investments by 'beating the market'. Two advisers, who are currently angling for my money, both claim they 'plan to achieve' seven per cent a year even though the long-term stock-market average is around five per cent. For this service, they both want over £3,000 of my money every year either directly in fees or indirectly in commissions. If you hear an adviser saying they can beat the market, it's worth remembering that in the City and on Wall Street around eighty per cent of professional investment managers supported by the brightest analysts and the most powerful computer systems fail to 'beat the market' year after year (see *Reason 24 – We put our trust in unit trusts*). But many financial advisers work for small firms with limited resources. Unlike the major investment companies, they do not have hundreds of financial analysts and millions of pounds of complex computer systems constantly scouring the market for above-average opportunities. So how a local firm with just a few employees is going to achieve what some of the largest City and Wall Street institutions cannot do is something you should mull over before you let go of your money.

Financial advisers can perform some very important services for us. They can explain about how stock markets and investments work. After all, most of us probably aren't clear about the advantages and disadvantages of unit trusts versus investment trusts versus open ended investment companies (OEICs) versus exchange traded funds (ETFs). Financial advisers can also inform us about the risk levels of our investment decisions; tell us about the suitability of savings and investment products given our particular family and financial circumstances; and make recommendations as to which investments to consider and which to avoid. Some might even be able to tell us about the tax implications of various investment choices. They can also help us with the administration of our money and produce income and capital gains statements for tax authorities.

If you use a financial adviser for what they can do, you can get good value. If you believe that your financial adviser will somehow perform better than the best investment managers in the world, disappointment awaits.

Mistake 2 – We choose an adviser recommended by a friend

Few of us have the time or opportunity to interview four or five financial advisers to choose the one who we would trust or who best suits our needs. Even if we could interview a few, we would probably have difficulty sorting the wheat from the chaff, or in some towns even finding any wheat amongst the chaff. So we often have to fall back on recommendations from friends or colleagues. Sometimes this may be a valid approach – if a relative or a friend has been served well, then better the devil we know. But Bernie Madoff was an expert in using social networks to recruit new investors. As his victims found out, following the advice of those we know doesn't always ensure a financially pleasant experience. At least not for the investor. Of course, we should listen to the experiences of those we know and whose judgement we trust. But that should not mean that we don't do our own due diligence – visit the adviser's offices; meet all their staff; understand how their business works; question them about what they can and cannot do for us; check their qualifications and investigate whether they have ever had any complaints or court judgements against them. Advice from those we know can help us with our choice of financial adviser, but it should not be the only or main criteria in our decision.

Mistake 3 – We give a financial adviser control over our money

We have to be very clear about whether we are choosing a financial adviser who, as the title states, should give us financial advice or a wealth/money manager who will manage our money for us. With a financial adviser, we should remain in control of our money. If we decide to make a recommended investment, we should buy it taking advantage of whatever discounts the adviser can arrange for us. And any money from cashing in an investment should be paid directly to us, not into the adviser's bank account. Ideally we should never give a financial adviser authority to move our money, should never sign blank or partially completed documents and absolutely never use the adviser's mailing address as the main point of contact for any companies whose products we decide to buy.

If we are actually looking for a wealth manager to manage our money for us, then we usually have to give them legal authority to move our money as they see fit. But that is a completely different business from working with a financial adviser. A difficulty is that many financial advisers will claim that we cannot get discounts or other advantages unless we hand over management of our money to them. This often leads to savers allowing someone who should just be giving advice to become the legal executor of their savings. However much you trust your adviser, giving him or her control over your money may not be a smart thing to do. A particularly dangerous mistake some people make is to give a financial adviser power over the assets of an elderly relative who might not be sufficiently *compos mentis* to manage their own financial affairs. For more than obvious reasons, that way disaster lies.

Mistake 4 – We buy recommended investment 'opportunities'

There are very few real investment 'opportunities' – shares or commodities that are about to shoot up in price. Even if there were, it's rather unlikely that our financial adviser would be in the charmed inner circle of those well-connected usually multimillionaires who are in the know. Of course, there may be certain sectors like emerging markets or healthcare or commodities like gold or oil, which are likely to outperform the market for a short period until they attract so much investor money that they become overpriced. But we should be very careful when a financial adviser recommends a particular share or other investment that is supposedly about to either rocket or even just drift up in value. Usually these recommended investments pay high levels of commissions to the adviser. But they may be in smaller companies whose shares can be difficult to sell or else are in complex financial products which are profitable for the adviser rather than for us.

There are plenty of shares, unit trusts and other investments that are in well-known companies, are widely traded and are simple to understand. There should be no need for ordinary savers and investors to stray away from mass-market, widely-available shares and savings products and take a punt on some dubious company or scheme recommended by an overly eager adviser.

Mistake 5 – We hire the organ-grinder but the monkey manages our money

Many financial adviser firms will use their best or most experienced people to sweet-talk us into becoming their clients. Many will operate an 'eat what you kill' bonus scheme – each partner or manager's year-end bonus will be directly linked to the amount of money they personally bring in and the fees they extract from this money. But all the time an adviser's top guns spend hunting and catching new clients means less time used for ensuring existing clients get the best investment advice. Very often we are persuaded to buy a financial adviser's services by the man (or woman) with the grey hair and years of experience, but the actual management of our money is done by a much less experienced, more junior member of their staff – we buy from the organ-grinder, but the monkey manages our money.

Mistake 6 – We use an adviser out of vanity or idleness

Many of us don't actually need a financial adviser. We unfortunately don't have enough money to make it worthwhile handing several thousand pounds a year either directly in fees or indirectly in commissions to someone else for something we mostly could do ourselves. For example, if we want exposure to stock markets we could put money into a cheap index-tracker fund (see *Reason 27 – We underestimate the power of inactivity*). Or else we could simply buy the top ten largest shares in any stock-market index. If we're looking for a savings account or an annuity, there are plenty of price comparison websites which will give us the 'best buys'. If we need somewhere for our pension savings, we are often just as likely as our adviser to guess which companies are going to achieve the best performance over the next twenty to thirty years. And if we wish to move our pension savings from an expensive provider to a cheaper one there are only four or five forms to fill in – doing it ourselves could save us thousands of pounds. But if we can't be bothered, the company receiving our pension money will probably do the paperwork for us, again avoiding the need to shove thousands of pounds of our savings into a financial adviser's pockets.

It's more common than we would like to think for people to hire a financial adviser because it makes them feel important or because all their friends have one. Others may just be too lazy to do some of the basic footwork for themselves. If you need a financial adviser, by all means hire one. But if you don't really need one, it can be an expensive luxury and not the best use of your money. Ten years of paying a financial adviser can easily cost you £30,000 to £50,000 either directly in fees or indirectly in commissions taken off your savings. You might have better uses for your money – if you don't, then you're welcome to give some of it to me. I need it.

Mistake 7 – We don't know how much they really cost

Perhaps the worst sin of all is that many of the savers who probably contribute over £16 billion a year to Britain's financial advisers probably don't even know exactly how much they personally are paying their adviser. Because so many advisers are being paid with complex combinations of upfront commissions, trailing commissions and discounts linked to the volumes of products they sell, most of their customers haven't a clue how much of their money is really going into the pockets of their financial adviser. It's never a good idea to buy something when you don't know how much you are paying, yet millions of us apparently do it when employing the services of a financial adviser.

Part 3

Investing – our pain, others' gain?

Reason 18

We think stock markets will always rise

A message we are constantly being given by people in financial services, investment pundits and personal finance journalists is that over the medium to long term, stock markets will always rise. So, although there might be some pretty astounding leaps and gut-wrenchingly horrific collapses over a couple of years, by the time we've held shares or unit trusts for five or more years we should normally see these increase significantly in value. Like much accepted wisdom used to encourage us to give our money to other people, this claim that markets will always rise is worth questioning.

Looking good

Looking at any chart of US, European or UK stock markets over the last century or so, the trend seems pretty clear – in spite of a bit of jumping around, the direction of travel is mostly upwards (see Figure 1)

So the conclusion is fairly obvious - only a madman or a fool would walk away from such an easy and low-risk way of making their savings grow. Unfortunately, life is seldom so simple.

Eaten by inflation

When showing stock-market growth and when telling us that we can earn eight or nine per cent a year or even more from shares, financial salespeople and pundits tend not to mention the effects of inflation. Taking account of inflation can make an impressive difference to the often exaggerated claims made about stock-market performance (see Figure 2).

Figure 1 – Long-term charts make it look as if stock markets almost always go up (Dow Jones Industrial Average)

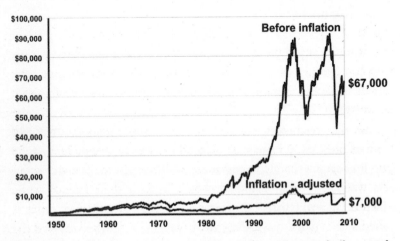

Figure 2 – Inflation wipes out most of the gains made by stock markets (S&P 500)

Using Figure 2, the US S&P 500 index would have turned $1,000 into around $67,000 over the last sixty years (top line on the chart) – a rise of around seven per cent a year. But once you cut out inflation, the $1,000 actually becomes about $7,000 (lower line on the chart). Over the whole period, inflation has eaten away $60,000 (around 89 per cent) of the apparent increase in an investor's wealth.

In Britain, the FTSE All-Share Index would have transformed £1,000 into £169,000 since it started in 1963. But knock out the effects of inflation and the real increase drops to just £12,000. Here inflation has gobbled up over ninety per cent of the supposed rise in value. So when someone is trying to tempt you into shares, a unit trust or some other stock-market investment by showing mouth-watering examples of how much you could have earned, you need to check whether the touted returns are before or after inflation – there is an awful lot of difference between the two. An inflation rate of just a few per cent may seem small, but over longer periods it can devour almost all of your potential profits.

Discarding the dead

When we are given the results of long-term stock-market performance, it's a bit like being given the results of all the people who completed a marathon. We may be told that the average time for all the runners was three hours or four hours or whatever. However, this probably only includes those who completed the course. The average times will not cover those who dropped out from exhaustion, had heart attacks on the way or stopped off at the pub for some welcome refreshment and then decided to stay there and watch the rest of the race on TV with their friends while downing a few pints. The marathon results would have what is called a 'survivors' bias'. Only the times of those who survived the race are reported.

Similarly, most stock-market indices have a survivors' bias

which makes the results appear better than the real performance of the underlying shares. For example, in an All-Share index, companies that have gone bankrupt disappear from the index. Yet if an ordinary investor had money in many of the shares, they would have been hit by any bankruptcies. With indexes of the top-performing shares like the FTSE 100, FTSE 250 or S&P 500, the survivors' bias has an even more significant effect. These indices are continually being adjusted as successful growing companies join them and shrinking failing companies are dropped off the radar. So, the index is measuring the most successful companies, not the average of all companies. This survivors' bias probably inflates apparent performance by less than one per cent a year, but it is still worth bearing in mind when the overall market may only be delivering around two to three per cent.

Boom boom

If you look at the long-term performance of US stocks, you can almost split the last hundred and thirty years into two main periods – 1880 to 1980 during which the market rose by less than one per cent a year (in real terms after taking out inflation) and the 1980 to 2010 boom when the index shot up by around four per cent a year (see Figure 3).

Over the whole 110 years the real (inflation-adjusted) rise in the index was about 1.5 per cent a year. As we look to the future to imagine what will happen to markets over the next ten to twenty years, we have to make a decision – do we expect markets to follow the long-term trend of around 1.5 per cent a year? Do we think growth will be nearer what happened in the last thirty years – a rise of about four per cent a year? Will it be somewhere in between? Are we in for years of economic stagnation with little to no growth? Or could prices be heading for a fall?

A rational optimist would probably argue that the 1980 to 2010 boom in stock markets was driven by things like rising wealth, increasing population and expansion of global trade which have led to greater company profits and more money going into stock markets. With continued rising life expectancy, improvements in the standards of living of hundreds of millions in developing countries and a flood of savings from more recently industrialised (especially Asian) countries, the future possibly looks bright for any money put into share-linked investments and pension savings.

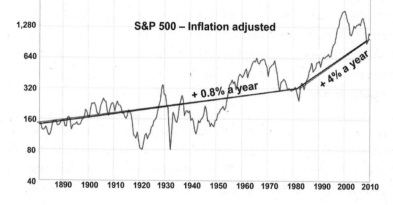

Figure 3 – Markets rose quite slowly until the 1980s then there was a boom

However, a rational pessimist might attribute the 1980 to 2010 boom to two main causes – baby boomers and debt-based consumption.

The baby boomers have probably been the luckiest and most affluent generation in human history. The huge baby-boomer generation (people born between 1945 and 1965) reached their peak earning and saving potential in the last thirty years. It's possible that the stock-market boom has been fuelled by a tsunami of baby-boomer money moving into shares and pensions savings. As the baby boomers now approach retirement, they will transition from being earners and savers to becoming non-earners and spenders. When pension companies have to start paying out the baby boomers' pensions, this could lead to their money being withdrawn from stock markets and placed in safer investments like government bonds. One estimate puts the likely withdrawal rate for the US at $1.7 trillion a year. With the total value of US shares being around $15 trillion, over ten per cent being taken out each year could cause a massive collapse in share prices. The US Government Accountability Office has produced a report claiming that there will not be a massive withdrawal of baby boomer funds from shares, mutual funds and pension savings and so everything will be all right. However, this view does not take account of what happens in real life where greed and panic can cause huge rises and falls that are not always justified by the underlying state of the economy. If a tipping point is reached where the withdrawal of some baby-boomer money causes a significant fall in share prices, then there could be a panic as other baby boomers and the pension funds holding their money rush to protect the value of their investments. If $2 trillion, $3 trillion or even more is quickly pulled out of shares, the results are not going to be pretty for anyone left with their savings still stuck in the market.

The second reason for worrying about future market performance is the increasing levels of government and personal debt. In the US, government debt shot up from less than $4 trillion in the 1980s to over $13 trillion by 2010. In Britain, debt rocketed from £200 billion to above £900 billion. In some Mediterranean countries the increasing debt figures go off the scale and several countries are to all intents and purposes bankrupt owing much more than they can ever pay back. Household debt has also shown similar growth. This increasing debt has pumped money into the economy thus driving economic activity and share prices above the level they would normally have achieved. So the 1980 to 2010 stock-market boom may have been partly fuelled by government and personal borrowing. At some point, governments and families are going to have to stop increasing debt and even begin to pay down their unprecedented levels of borrowing. This could result in a huge withdrawal of money from the economy and a collapse in company profits which would also bring down share prices.

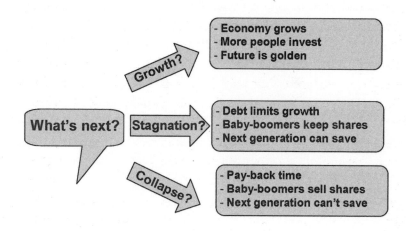

Figure 4 – It's not certain that shares will continue to increase in value

It is possible that the gradual rise in stock markets from 1880 to 1980 was based on real growth in production and living standards, but that the last thirty years of boom have mainly been a debt-fuelled, baby boomer, 'let's-have-it-all' party. If this is true, then the future for any money in shares may not look too wonderful. So the question we all have to ask as financial advisers, unit trusts, banks and pension companies try to persuade us to trust them with our money is: what will the next decade or two bring? Will it be continued company profits leading to rising share prices? Or will we see economic stagnation as governments milk taxpayers to pay down national debt? Or could there be a collapse in stock markets when the baby-boomers withdraw their savings from shares, families reduce borrowing and we find that the next generation has insufficient money to prop up share prices because it is laden with debt and has little if anything to put into savings? (see Figure 4)

The answer is not obvious. But if a financial professional is trying to get hold of your savings and cannot give a well-reasoned explanation about why there won't be either stagnation or a rout, then you should be quite wary.

Reason 19

We invest looking in the rear-view mirror

As we look at or are shown charts and figures illustrating stock-market growth, we're looking backwards at what happened in the past. Financial sellers and ads usually warn us that 'past performance is no guide to the future', but the way our brains work means we are always trying to find patterns in events and series of figures. So, in spite of the warnings, we tend to extrapolate any past trends into the future. After all, if a unit trust is shooting up in value, we assume the fund manager must be doing something right and will continue to do so. Or if a stock market is rocketing up we imagine that there must be a good reason and so it's time for us to jump on the bandwagon. That's why sellers will big up how well certain funds or products have performed or how much markets have risen in the past. They show us that something has gone up with the implication that it will continue to go up. They know that our search for meaningful trends will cause most of us to disregard the warnings they are legally obliged to give us about past performance not indicating what will happen in the future.

But making investment decisions while looking at past data is a bit like driving while only looking at the rear-view mirror. It's as if we're going up a hill and, looking backwards, we see the road is going upwards and assume the road will continue to climb. In fact, of course, the opposite will always happen – the higher we drive up a hill, the more likely it is that we will reach the top and soon start descending.

Stock markets behave in a similar way. The higher they rise, the more likely they are to fall. The standard stock-market figures and charts we're usually shown make it look like markets regularly go up. It's true that there is a very slow upwards drift of stock market indices of around one per cent a year with perhaps another half a per cent due to the effects of survivors' bias. Those charts and figures which suggest larger rises do so either because they don't take out the effects of inflation and/or because they show how much our savings will be worth including reinvesting dividends. But these disguise the fact that stock markets always return to an extremely slowly rising long-term average level in what's called 'reversion to the mean'. We can best see this if we look at the long-term price/earnings (P/E) ratio (the price of shares compared to their earnings). This shows that markets move around an average level (see Figure 1).

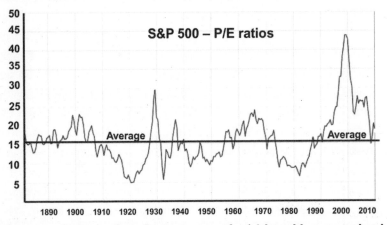

Figure 1 – Many markets fluctuate around a fairly stable average level

In this case I've used the S&P 500 Index. Here the average P/E is somewhere between fifteen and sixteen. For the FTSE, the long-term P/E ratio is about thirteen. If we view shares in this way, then we should see that the higher a share's P/E or the overall market's P/E, then the more likely it is to fall in the future. And, of course, the lower the P/E ratio, the more probable it is that it will rise unless the company or the economy is in trouble. When driving a car we look forward and see that the nearer we are to a high point, the closer the next descent is. In the same way, when being offered an investment which is shooting up in value, we should look forward to the likely reversion to the mean and expect a fall and not just look back at the rising trend. This is extremely difficult to do for two main reasons. Firstly, because it demands that we act contrary to the patterns that our minds form from any past data we are given. Secondly, because it means that we should invest in things when their value has fallen below the long-term average and sell them when values are rising above the long-term average. To translate P/Es back into the stock-market figures most of us see in the papers or hear on the news, a rough rule of thumb might suggest that it would be foolish to put any money into shares when the FTSE is above around 5,700 or the Dow Jones is much above about 10,000 (Figure 2).

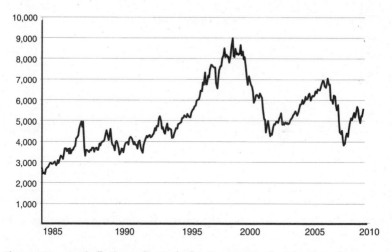

Figure 2 – An inflation-adjusted chart suggests that buying shares or unit trusts when the FTSE is above 5,700 might not be too smart

But, of course, I may be completely wrong. I usually am, otherwise I would have been wealthy long ago.

Experienced and successful investors talk about 'buying low, selling high' or buying when there is blood in the street and selling when everyone is partying to celebrate their gains. This goes against many of our natural instincts as most of us feel more comfortable buying when prices are shooting up and rush to sell when prices collapse. But if we can change from investing by looking in the rear-view mirror to navigating by what we see in front of us, then we can use an expectation of a reversion to the mean to avoid the fatal mistake made by over ninety per cent of savers who eagerly buy when the market is too high and are panicked into selling at a loss when prices drop.

Reason 20

We believe shares always outperform cash

Would you believe it?

In an article in a major national newspaper, a personal finance journalist gushed that if someone had invested just one pound in the stock market eighty years ago, it would be worth over £70,000 today. So £1,000 would have grown to a stunning £70 million. And in a book about investing, a writer explained that if you placed just £100 a month in shares between the ages of twenty and forty, you'd be a multimillionaire by the time you retired. Similar claims of the wealth created by stock markets are constantly repeated by personal finance journalists, investment companies, writers of books on investing and other financial insiders as they try to convince us that shares are the best investment we can make as they will always outperform things like bonds or cash deposits in a bank. Often these pundits will back up their prediction of the vast riches to be earned in stocks and shares by using what may be the most misleading chart ever shown to us ordinary investors (see Figure 1).

It is true that one pound put into US, UK or European shares in 1900 would have grown to around £90,000 by 2011. However, extending this trend, if one of your long dead forefathers had shoved £1,000 into shares in 1900 and you could keep your grubby hands off it, by the end of this century your children's children's children would have a stupendous £8,000,000,000 (eight billion pounds) or so to spend on a few of life's little luxuries. Not bad for a mere thousand quid invested at the beginning of the 1900s.

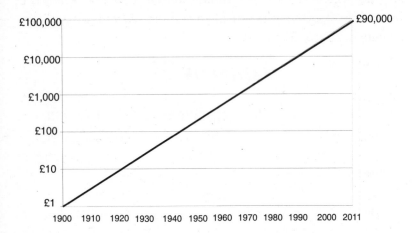

Figure 1 – We're often shown charts showing that money invested in shares increases enormously in value over the long term

Of course, these claims of vast easy wealth and the charts that seem to support them are at best misleading and at worst deliberately dishonest. For a start, they don't take account of the ravages of inflation. If we do Figure 1 again showing how much the one pound investment would be worth in real, not inflated, money, the results are much more modest – a few hundred pounds rather than £90,000. In fact over 99% of the touted gains from shares are wiped out by inflation over the very long term (see Figure 2).

But there is another problem with this chart and many similar ones that we are often shown. They are drawn with what is called a logarithmic scale - the vertical axis goes up by a factor of ten each time from one to ten to a hundred and so on. This makes it look like your money will grow both rapidly and at a regular rate and thus suggests that even if you don't keep it in shares for over a century, you'll still get lots back. But if I redraw Figure 2 using a normal scale, then you'll see that your money actually grows incredibly slowly. The line showing the increase in value before inflation only really starts to rise after about fifty to sixty years. As for the lines showing gains once the effects of inflation are taken away – they rise by so little that during the hundred and ten years they don't even seem to move (see Figure 3).

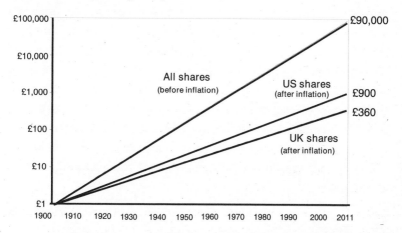

Figure 2 – When you take account of inflation, most of the supposed gains disappear

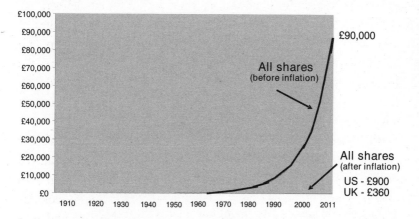

Figure 3 – Growth over the first fifty to sixty years is almost minimal

Charts like Figures 1 and 2 potentially give a deceptively overly-positive impression of how money invested in stock markets will grow. Yet they are widely used to encourage us to put our savings and pension money into stock-market investments. Then when you consider that most of us will only invest for twenty to thirty years at most and that very few of us will have significant quantities of money in shares, unit trusts and pension savings for fifty to a hundred years, we can forget about most of the wonderful stories of what has happened to shares over the last half century or more – the glorious upward trajectory of the top line on Figure 3. Instead we should focus on what's likely to happen in the ten, twenty or possibly thirty years we may hold shares either directly by buying them or investing in unit trusts or indirectly when our pension fund managers buy them. That means looking at the lower lines on Figure 3 – the ones you can't actually see because they don't really take off from the horizontal axis.

The modest truth

Most serious financial insiders will admit that the real returns from stock markets have been around five per cent above inflation. That compares very favourably to government and corporate bonds which have given about 1.8 per cent and to cash deposits which have yielded around 1.5 per cent. However, stock markets' five per cent is made up of two parts. Historically markets have gone up by somewhere around 1.5 per cent a year above the rate of inflation which is about the same as you would get from cash and has reflected the rate that company earnings have increased. Where shares outclass other investments is in the dividends companies pay to their shareholders which have averaged around 3.5 per cent a year provided they are reinvested and not spent. So, together the market growth and reinvested dividends give about a five per cent return.

There are two warnings to take from this. Firstly, anyone trying to flog you some investment which is linked to the rise in a stock-market index and doesn't include the dividends paid on the underlying shares is knowingly and cynically having a very profitable laugh at your expense. There have been quite a few banks selling unwitting customers so-called 'guaranteed bonds' which promise to pay anything from two thirds to 135 per cent of any rise in a stock market index and also magnanimously guarantee to refund all your capital if the stock market falls. These have been phenomenally successful with customers who haven't understood that most of the medium- to long-term (three or more years) gains from stock markets come from dividends, not from the rise in the level of the market index. So these people are being taken for mugs. There are few things which are certain in the world of savings and investments. But one is that the only real guarantee that these customers have is that, when they eventually get their money back, its purchasing power will be lower than when they originally handed it over.

The second warning is that we should be more than wary when financial insiders show us how much money we'll make assuming growth rates of seven or ten or even twelve per cent. Shares, savings, pension funds or whatever unfortunately don't grow by seven, ten or even twelve per cent. They give a return of around five per cent before tax and this is only after you include reinvesting the dividends. So you can usefully ignore anybody touting some savings or investment scheme claiming growth of substantially above five per cent a year. There was a hectic period of about twenty years from 1980 till the dotcom crash when stocks did achieve double-digit growth. But two things were happening. Firstly, there was a flood of baby-boomer cash chasing after somewhere to invest meaning that buyers outnumbered sellers which naturally pushed prices up. Secondly, it was a period of high inflation. In real terms, markets only rose by about seven per cent a year during the twenty years of madness. In the last decade, most stock markets have given zero or a negative return, bringing the longer-term yield back to the historical average of about five per cent.

Money in my pocket?

But even if you are realistic when you stick some money in shares, a unit trust or a pension and you accept that you'll probably get nearer five per cent rather than the exaggerated projections made by those who want your cash, a crucial question is: can you actually ever get the five per cent for yourself?

For a start, if you or your fund manager has to buy shares, you've already lost perhaps up to half a per cent in dealing costs and another half per cent in tax. Moreover, if you or your fund manager like to be frightfully active and continually buy and sell shares ostensibly to improve your returns, you'll be losing probably more than one per cent every time either of you makes a trade. In addition, if you have a financial adviser helping you choose shares, funds or a pension, then there's at least another one per cent going into someone else's pocket. And if your money is being managed by a unit trust or pension-fund manager, you can also kiss goodbye to anything from one per cent to three per cent in management fees and other costs. Plus, if you've been sold the brilliant idea of investing in what's called a 'fund of funds' – a unit trust which invests in other unit trusts – then you'll be paying out two sets of management fees. That's very generous of you, but not something that's likely to add much to your future wealth. The more intermediaries there are between you and your money, the more people there are taking a cut for themselves. And when your maximum longer-term likely earnings are only going to be around five per cent a year for shares and less for bonds or other investments, liberally handing out what seems like a modest one per cent here and one per cent there is actually going to slaughter any real returns for you.

Yes, all the figures of past performance indicate that stock markets should give us about five per cent a year providing we can reinvest all our dividends. Yes, this is substantially more than we'll get from cash in a bank. But by the time quite a few people have taken their slice from our salami, there's often precious little left for us. When we then factor in the risk with stock markets that buying at the wrong time could mean our investments fall in value, the old adage that shares always outperform cash may be true for the overall market, but may not be true for millions upon millions of individual savers and investors whose potential gains end up in other people's already brimming bank accounts.

Reason 21

Only a mastermind or manipulator can predict the market

Look, it's quite simple

Those of us who regularly or even occasionally read the money pages or business pages of our newspapers, are frequently treated to articles telling us where to invest and where to avoid. We'll be told why China is the next big opportunity or why US shares are a disaster in the making or why pharma is the best bet or why we should buy defensive shares or why gold is the place to be or why high-interest bank accounts are pulling in all the smart money or why bank shares are overvalued and so on and so forth. Yet on the very same day it's possible to find journalists putting forward completely opposing views, both well argued and extremely convincing.

Yesterday I read two pieces, one telling me that US shares were about to shoot up by over thirty per cent because companies had reduced debts, had good cashflows and were reporting record profits. Seemed good to me and cheered me up for a few minutes until I read another sage predicting US stocks were set for a massive crash because the huge government stimulus hadn't worked, the economy was slowing, consumer demand was dropping, firms were shedding jobs, national debt was unsustainable and several states were bankrupt. Last week one pundit was prophesying further rises in the price of gold, but another was claiming it was overvalued and heading for a crash. Recently I chanced across an expert arguing that retail sales were strong with many shops showing increases over the previous year. Yet on the same day there was another specialist explaining that overall retail sales were dropping and only looked good because so many shops were closing down that the few survivors were getting a little extra business from their now bankrupt former competitors.

Part of the problem seems to be that in any situation there are sufficient indicators to prove almost anything. So it's easy for commentators to take whatever information suits their argument and to make a credible case for their point of view. Depending on who you read or listen to, on any one day you might well believe either the world is about to collapse into a deep depression or we're all about to become rich and happy. This does make decisions about where to put your money slightly more than complicated.

What moves markets?

There seem to be at least four main forces which drive the value of anything in which we might want to put our money:

- There's the fundamental value of a company or a bond. Naturally, top-performing companies and lower-risk bonds tend to be worth more than shares and bonds in badly-managed basket cases, whether they be companies or countries.
- Then we have to overlay the economic situation. In times of economic growth and prosperity, even dogs can shine; when the economy is tanking, even the best shares may not have many buyers and so prices fall.
- In addition to that, we need to take account of speculative behaviour. Massive investments or shorting by hedge funds and large traders, reinforced by them spreading false rumours and inaccurate stories can frequently distort the prices of individual shares, sectors or commodities wiping

out the suckers who thought that all you needed to do was to look at a company's profitability and the state of the economy before deciding what to buy.

- Finally we have human behaviour – what's called 'sentiment momentum' – savers' tendency to react with either ecstasy or anguish whenever the value of their investments either rises or falls.

At any time, these four forces can move in the same direction or in different and opposing directions. Unfortunately most commentators seize upon one or at most two of these forces when giving us the benefit of their genius and so what they propose seldom matches the complexity of real life and is usually proved to be misguided. Though, in the same way a broken clock is right twice a day, every pundit will occasionally have their successes which they will repeatedly shove in our faces, conveniently forgetting about their considerably more numerous failed forecasts.

Reducing our own returns

In the early twentieth century, the behaviour of ordinary savers was probably a significant influence on the movements of markets. However, nowadays most of us have handed over our money to professional middlemen like unit trust managers, pension funds and life insurance companies, so our behaviour probably has little effect on what happens to financial markets and share and bond prices. The actions of ordinary savers were once one of the strongest forces moving markets, but have now become one of the weakest.

Although we have almost no power to move markets, our behaviour does have the power to massively reduce any returns we get from the money we put into financial markets. Those people who actively manage their money are constantly being buffeted by a storm of contradictory opinions about where to put their cash. It's difficult to keep one's nerve if a distinguished financial journalist informs us, for example, that we are fools to keep our money in banking stocks or that we are idiots not to buy banking stocks. But by the time we read our weekend newspaper, any information we are getting is days old and market insiders will have already reacted to whatever trend the journalist is alerting us.

Studies of the behaviour of ordinary investors have shown that they repeatedly get much lower returns than the overall market can provide because they over-react to both good and bad news. One of the largest surveys done in the US showed that while the stock market managed to turn $10,000 into $48,000 over an eighteen year period, ordinary investors on average reduced the $10,000 to $9,000.

Typically we hear about something – gold prices rising, falling profits at entertainment companies, how buy-to-lets are a sure-fire way of saving for a pension, the great opportunities in corporate bonds or whatever. Then a short time later, the people we know may tell us that they've put money into what is 'hot' and they've done really well from it. So we take a look at what's happening and prices seem to be going up. Finally, we take the plunge and join the rush. A few weeks or months on, more people have joined the parade and prices have continued to rise. We feel pretty good about our decision and this reinforces our belief that we are above average, that we understood what was happening in the market and that we acted wisely. But soon the market where we put our money peaks, the insiders and first-movers bail out taking their profits and prices fall slightly. At first we're not too worried. We may not have lost much, in fact we may still be up. But some more insiders decide to jump ship and prices fall again. We're rattled but hold on in the expectation that prices will move up again. Then more people close to the action run for the hills and prices shoot down. We panic and sell at a loss in our rush for the exit (see Figure 1).

But rather than learning the lesson that the quickest way to lose money is to buy too high and then sell too low, most of us console ourselves with the fact that many other people were in the same boat as us and also lost money. So when the next hot thing comes along, we go back to square one and start the whole process again. Meanwhile, whatever it is that we sold at a loss has mysteriously gone up in value again. Moreover, many of us do what is called 'informationless investing' – we put money into something when we have that money from a bonus or pay rise or inheritance, rather than when there is a compelling reason to invest. It is unlikely that our receipt of funds will exactly coincide with a great investment opportunity and so we may well end up getting into something at the wrong time.

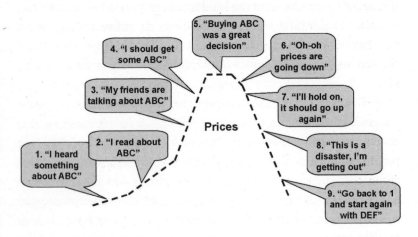

Figure 1 – Ordinary savers repeatedly destroy the value of their savings by buying too high and selling too low

So this is what to do

All this poses a bit of a problem for us ordinary savers. If everyone's rushing into gold or buy-to-lets or defensive shares, should we join the stampede believing that the price is bound to go up and that this is a great opportunity? Or should we take a contrarian view and stand aside expecting that there will be a price bubble that will burst when the early movers take their profits and mass panic ensues? Yet if we wait on the sidelines, we might miss the great opportunity and be forced to stand miserably in the corner while all our friends party after they make a packet.

Of course, the experts will tell us that we should do what's called 'market timing' - buy when prices of shares, commodities, properties or precious metals are low and sell when they are high. But how can we be sure when they actually are high or low? If we buy when prices are half-way through a fall, we're going to lose our shirts and trousers too. But if we sell too early during a rise, we'll see others become rich while we only make modest gains if we make anything at all. Market timing isn't easy. One study showed that over a period of seventy two years, if you'd misjudged the stock market on just five key days you'd have halved your returns. Only extremely good hindsight would have allowed you to identify those five critical days and by then it's a bit late.

If I or any of the other commentators really knew how to invest successfully, none of us would be telling you. The lesson here is that usually any situation is much more complicated than our favourite pundits would have us believe. Experts can find sufficient evidence to argue that prices of whatever investment they're discussing will either rise or stagnate or fall. And usually different experts can make each of these cases equally convincingly depending on which side of the bed they got out of that morning or on which investment, unit trust, bank account or pension plan they are being encouraged to promote or denigrate.

Many people do make vast fortunes playing the markets. There are a few geniuses who can understand markets and their names are well-known. There are market manipulators who will always make a killing by fleecing ordinary savers. And there are financial industry insiders who make fortunes by handling our savings and taking a cut every time they can get us to move our money. But for the rest of us, anticipating price movements and finding good investment opportunities is seldom quite as simple as many pundits and commentators often like to make out.

Reason 22

Vested interests usually talk up the market

Get in while you can

There is one common feature of every investment fashion and fad - there are always plenty of people with vested interests who get a lot of media space to talk up whatever's hot and making them money. It doesn't matter if it's the South Sea Company, Dutch tulips, shares, buy-to-lets, holiday homes, modern art, stuffed sharks, ostrich farms, gold, titanium, stamps, vintage cars or fine wines - wherever there's money to be made, there will be a flood of supposed experts and other cheerleaders enthusiastically encouraging us to follow the herd and put our money into the schemes they benefit from promoting. Just before the South Sea bubble burst in 1720, newspaper readers were encouraged to jump in, 'South Sea is all the rage and fashion and happy are they that are in'. A few months later another commentator described the bloody aftermath of the frenzied rush into South Sea Company shares, 'persons in all ranks in society were left penniless'. The apparent happiness of 'they that are in' didn't last too long and for many turned to complete ruin. Subsequent investigations revealed that the bubble had largely been a result of fraud, political corruption, false stories run in the press and stock price manipulation. Spool forward a couple of hundred years and ordinary people were once again being exhorted to entrust their savings to financial insiders in the great 1920s stock-market bonanza. Here, even as prices began to wobble and crash, financiers and politicians were still urging the masses to jump on the bandwagon (see Figure 1).

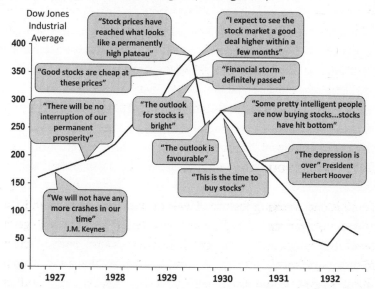

Figure 1 – In the 1920s and 1930s, vested interests lured ordinary people to risk and lose their savings while many financial insiders and politicians walked away with millions

Needless to say, as with the South Sea Bubble, persons in all ranks of society were left penniless and subsequent investigations revealed that much of the bubble had been a result of our recurring old friends - fraud, political corruption, false stories run in the press and massive stock price manipulation.

There were several other booms and busts in the twentieth century, the biggest probably being the dotcom one. At the time, to its credit *The Economist* suggested that 'America is experiencing a serious asset bubble'. But *The New York Times* derided anyone talking about a bubble accusing them of trying 'to find a bubble worth worrying about' while *The Wall Street Journal* described those predicting a collapse as experiencing 'extreme paranoia about imaginary future disasters'. Meanwhile various experts breathlessly informed us that, 'a new order is building that obeys a different set of rules' and 'hang on to your hat and smash your crystal ball, the world is changing as you read these words'.

Unfortunately, the world wasn't really changing that much after all and anyone tempted into dotcom stocks really did have to hang on their hats as they soon saw a large part or all of their money evaporate. Again, the result was penniless people and subsequent revelations that once again a significant part of the boom was a result of fraud, political corruption, false stories run in the press and stock price manipulation. More recently we have been told that, 'prospective returns from equities are at the most attractive levels seen for some 20 years in the US and over 25 years in Europe and the UK' and that, 'history says fill your boots, sell your wife, dive in' and 'buy now while stocks are low'.[27] Perhaps. Or perhaps not. But in general, history does suggest that the more enthusiastic a commentator, journalist or financial adviser is, the more wary an ordinary saver should be.

Cui bono?

Time and again, we seem to forget that there is nobody in financial services who is working primarily for our benefit. Analysts, advisers, journalists, pundits – they're not charity workers. Understandably they're all out to make the best living they can for themselves and their families. If they really knew how to make money investing, they wouldn't be wasting their time and energy telling us. They'd be cashing in and counting their many millions. Everybody writing and talking about where you should put your money has a vested interest. Of course, we should listen to the analyses and prognostications of genuine experts and some insiders. We might learn something useful. But we should also question why they are so generously giving us the benefit of their apparent knowledge because their motives may not always be as pure as we would hope.

Reason 23

Stock markets may be rigged against us

Trust in me

Any stock market can only survive if ordinary savers feel they have a reasonable chance of making a gain on their investments in shares, unit trusts or pension savings. If we lose confidence in the fairness of markets and start to believe they are rigged against us, then we're unlikely to risk our savings in a game where we suspect we have no chance of winning. If trust disappears, prices collapse due to a lack of buyers and either the market is destroyed or else it can take years before we can be tempted back in. In 2002, for example, the German small companies market, Neuer Markt, was closed down completely after prices fell by around ninety five per cent following revelations of massive stock-price manipulation and fraud by insiders. After the 1929 US market crash, it took over thirty years until sufficient investors were coaxed back into the market to push shares back up to their pre-1929 level. And following the dotcom fiasco, share prices stayed flat for ten years as many savers put their money into things like property rather than risking getting burnt once again by over-hyped, over-inflated and outrageously manipulated share prices. Unfortunately, so much money flowed into property that there was an unprecedented housing price bubble which eventually burst causing losses for many savers and almost destroying the financial system.

"The investing public is sceptical and rightly so. It's

no surprise that people are staying away from stocks. There has been an accumulation of blows from Bernie Madoff, the financial crisis, bail-out of Wall Street and flash crash that feeds into a perception, rightly or wrongly, that the game is rigged."[28]

It's vital for stock markets' survival that ordinary savers believe in the basic integrity of markets. So, most stock markets claim that they have established regulatory systems that protect ordinary savers and ensure a level playing field balancing the interests of outsiders with those of insiders. However, there is increasing evidence that this self-regulation is ineffective, that the main markets are heavily rigged against ordinary savers and that insiders are getting obscenely rich at our expense.

If you knew what I knew

The most basic advantage insiders like traders and brokers have is that they learn about any new information affecting share prices long before we, our unit trust managers or our pension fund managers find out something is up. So the insiders can buy or sell well in advance of the general public and even those who manage our savings. Theoretically, this constitutes insider dealing and is illegal. But it is seldom discovered and even when discovered it is rarely prosecuted. After all, stock markets fear loss of public confidence from the publicity surrounding insider dealing much more than they care about a few people making millions defrauding ordinary savers.

"Many clients sat on the boards of public companies and were more than happy to brief us about their own shares. They used coded signals and texts to get the message out that the time was right to buy or sell their stock before the public got hold of the information."[29]

When rampant insider dealing is discovered, usually everything is quickly swept under the carpet signalling to insiders that they can do whatever they want as long as they don't get caught. Unlike mugging or burglary, insider dealing may at first sight seem like a victimless crime. But we are the victims. Every hundred million extracted through insider dealing is a hundred million taken directly from us or from our savings and pensions. It is theft on a massive scale and it is theft that normally goes undetected and even when accidentally detected is almost never punished. This makes it one of the easiest, virtually risk-free ways of becoming fantastically wealthy.

Pumped, pooped and plundered

While trading on insider information is supposedly illegal yet seldom punished, using smart tricks to manipulate share prices is less obviously frowned upon. There are several techniques insiders use to profit from share price movements at our expense. Churn-and-burners increase their commissions through excessive buying and selling of their clients' portfolios making themselves money with each transaction while simultaneously reducing their clients' wealth. With many unit trusts increasing the percentage of their holdings they trade each year from thirty per cent in 2007, to fifty per cent in 2008 to almost ninety per cent now, one could be forgiven for suspecting that managers are making themselves and their brokers rich by churning-and-burning our money.

With pump-and-dump (also called 'ramping'), insiders buy up shares in a target company and spread rumours of upcoming good news about the company or else get helpful analysts to issue 'buy' recommendations. When others rush in to seize this 'opportunity' the price goes up and the pump-and-dumpers get rid of their shares, banking a tidy profit.

Poop-and-scoop is the opposite of pump-and-dump. The poop-and-scooper uses false or exaggerated information or 'sell' recommendations to drive down the price of a share. They then buy up shares at the lower price and make money selling when the share drifts back up to its normal price. Short-and-distort is similar with the difference that insiders also short shares before pushing the price down.

Then once you add in other methods like circular trading, jitney, dividend pumping, double-dipping and bucketing, you're virtually guaranteeing that insiders will always make very healthy profits at the expense of outsiders.

It's a fun game, it's a lucrative game

The profits to be made from pushing share prices up or down a few per cent are limited by the amount of money an insider has to buy the shares whose prices they are manipulating. But potential profits can be massive when insiders leverage their money so that they can take huge positions with quite modest sums. They can, for example, use spread betting where it's not uncommon to earn thirty to fifty times the money bet. Or else insiders can work like hedge funds by borrowing massively to take speculative positions gambling on specific share-price movements.

The huge extent of this price manipulation was revealed in an interview with a former hedge-fund manager who then became a financial pundit. He explained that if a hedge fund had taken a short position on a stock (i.e. bet that the price would fall) and what he called 'pay-day' was coming, then the fund couldn't afford to let the market rise. As he said, 'it's critically important to use a lot of your firepower' to lower prices.

> **"I would encourage anyone in the hedge fund business to do it because it's legal and it's a very quick way to make money and it's satisfying."**

He would apparently throw about $5 million to $10 million into bringing prices down, spread a few negative stories by ringing up a few brokers and use what he called the 'bozos' on the main financial papers to orchestrate a fall in the stock's price. He went on to explain, 'these are all the things you must do day-to-day and if you're not doing them, maybe you shouldn't be in the game'. Similarly, if he had gone long on a stock (bet that the price would rise), he would spread imaginative stories to push the price up. Investment specialists will continually tell us that the price of shares is linked to the fundamental value of companies being traded. But this former hedge fund manager claimed that 'the mechanics' (the way he could manipulate share prices to make huge amounts of money) were much more important to share price movements than 'the fundamentals' (the real underlying value of the shares).

Fast money, easy money, our money

A more recent development which is enabling well-funded insiders to profit while outsiders lose is called 'high-frequency trading'. The big trading houses and banks have developed powerful computer algorithms that can scan the main marketplaces, identify the buy and sell orders before they are carried out and then execute millions of orders a second just ahead of the orders coming into the market. It's the ultimate in gambling certainty. It's like betting on thousands of horse races when you already know all the results. You can't possibly lose. High frequency traders know exactly what's going to happen to a share price, including how much buyers are prepared to pay and at what price sellers will sell, after the buy and sell orders are launched but before they are executed. By exploiting this knowledge they will always be able to make easy profits.

"This (high-frequency trading) is where all the money is getting made. If an individual investor doesn't have the means to keep up, they're at a huge disadvantage."[30]

One research group estimated that high-frequency trading was giving profits of over $20 billion a year in the US. And that $20 billion or more is money that comes directly from the investment returns that would otherwise have gone to ordinary savers and investors in unit trusts and pensions. High-frequency trading has further reinforced what has increasingly become a two-tier market which makes insiders wealthy while working against ordinary investors in shares, unit trusts and pensions.

Between a rock and a hard place

With cash savings and bonds giving such poor returns, there seems to be nowhere else we can put our savings apart from stock markets, either through shares, unit trusts or pension funds. We ordinary investors might make a little money from stock markets over the medium to longer term. But there are many indications that the markets are massively rigged in favour of insiders who make millions while leaving just a few scraps on the table for us outsiders. Moreover, all this is happening in supposedly well regulated US and European markets. The abuses that are going on daily in the Wild East – Russia, India, China and other Third World stock exchanges – don't bear thinking about.

Reason 24

We put our trust in unit trusts

Along with credit cards and ATMs, unit trusts are probably one of the best financial innovations of the last sixty years. Unit trusts have been described as 'a breakthrough in financial democracy' because they have enabled ordinary savers to get access to professional financial management at very low cost. Before the development of unit trusts, most of us would have had to buy shares in individual companies if we wanted exposure to stock markets. Unit trusts allowed us to pool our money with other savers to then be invested by fund management experts in various combinations of shares, bonds and cash. This removed much of the hard work and uncertainty for us as we no longer had to analyse companies' performance or the advantages and disadvantages of different bonds before deciding where to invest – the fund managers and their staff did this for us. The ease and low cost of putting money into unit trusts has encouraged many people to save. In fact, for possibly the majority of savers, unit trusts have long been the most sensible, productive and efficient way to grow their money. However, what started as a breakthrough which has benefited tens of millions of savers may now have become a huge and immensely profitable colossus that no longer works in our interests.

Breeding like rabbits

The unit trust industry has seen enormous growth. In the US (where they're called 'mutual funds'), there were only about four hundred mutuals in 1970 managing around $30 billion. Now there are over six thousand funds with more than $3 trillion invested in them. In Britain, another six thousand or so funds manage in excess of £500 billion of our money.

In the early days of unit trusts they simplified investment decisions for us - we could choose from a few hundred funds and they would weed out the wheat from the chaff amongst the many thousands of publicly-listed companies to find the best places to put our savings. But now we are in an almost ludicrous situation where there are more funds than there are companies for them to invest in. By 2011 there were around 6,300 funds based in the US of which about 3,840 were domestic funds channelling US savers' money into just 2,900 stocks listed on the NYSE. There are around 6,300 funds operating out of Britain. Of these we can choose from more than 3,200 to put money in only about 2,600 companies on the London Stock Exchange, AIM and Techmark markets. Globally there are in the region of fifteen thousand companies which attract unit trust and mutual fund money and yet we have over eighteen thousand funds competing for our cash to invest in those fifteen thousand companies. This means that many funds are forced to buy the same shares. If you look at the prospectuses from, for example, the main UK unit trusts, their top ten investments are mostly in the same companies – HSBC, Aviva, GlaxoSmithKline, Vodafone, Centrica, AstraZenica, Tesco and so on. So it has almost become simpler for us to go back to buying shares in a few larger individual companies directly rather than trying to choose between the many thousands of unit trusts and mutual funds all eager to manage our cash.

Making off with our money

At first sight, the unit trust costs of two to three per cent that individual savers pay may appear quite modest. But funds manage such huge sums that their charges aggregate up to massive amounts of money taken from our savings each year. In the US, where charges are slightly lower, savers pay in the region of $45 billion to $75 billion a year to mutuals – $176 million to $294 million a day – to look after their investments. In Britain we cough up £10 billion to £15 billion a year – £40 million to £60 million a day. This £40 million to £60 million a day comes directly from our savings and has a terribly destructive impact on any returns we are likely to get.

Another way to look at the extraordinary costs of unit trusts is to say that as there are more unit trusts and mutual funds than there are companies to invest in, then each year the dealings in each company's shares must produce enough money to pay for the directors, managers, staff, offices and other costs of more than one unit trust before there is any money left over for ordinary investors. The idea of each publicly-listed company having to support the costs of more than one unit trust may help us visualise the almost unbelievable amounts of wealth being hoovered up by the unit trust and mutual fund industry each year at the expense of companies and savers.

Big isn't beautiful

Perhaps the most worrying development in the unit trust industry is how it has moved away from being a business where a limited number of funds tried to provide effective, low-cost financial management and has instead become more akin to consumer mass marketing where all that seems to matter for thousands of funds is getting in as much investor money as possible to maximise profits for fund management firms.

Many unit trusts follow a similar life cycle. A fund is started with say thirty or fifty million pounds or dollars or euros. Because it is managing a relatively small amount of money, it can flexibly pursue the best investment opportunities and so tends to outperform older, larger and less flexible funds. Moreover in the early stages of their life, the key priority for most funds is to demonstrate rapid growth as this is what will draw in more savers' money.

Gradually the unit trust attracts more funds as financial advisers recommend it to their clients and its assets grow to maybe a hundred or two hundred million. A year or so later, the management company takes out big press adverts trumpeting the fund's extraordinary success. This attracts a flood of new money as ordinary savers pile in, completely ignoring the legally compulsory warning, 'Past performance is no guide to the future'. Studies have repeatedly shown that most new investor money goes into the top-performing funds, particularly those advertised in the press and investing publications. Soon the fund may have five hundred, seven hundred or even a billion pounds, dollars or euros under management.

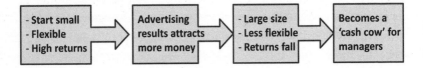

- Start small
- Flexible
- High returns

Advertising results attracts more money

- Large size
- Less flexible
- Returns fall

Becomes a 'cash cow' for managers

Figure 1 – As unit trusts grow, their performance tends to decline

Now growth becomes a bit more difficult. In most of the world's stock exchanges, the 80/20 rule applies – eighty per cent of the value of shares is accounted for by just twenty per cent of the largest companies. Sometimes it's even more like a 90/10 rule. When unit trusts have smaller sums to manage, they can focus on smaller and medium-sized companies with the best growth prospects. But as the amount of money managed by trusts goes up, they have more money than there are opportunities to invest in. It's generally accepted that any new information about a company is known to all the main players in a market within less than an hour. When a unit trust just has thirty or fifty million under management, it can sometimes achieve high returns by spotting the occasional opportunity. But when it has five hundred million or more, there simply aren't sufficient opportunities for such large sums and it increasingly has to buy the shares of the larger companies in each country – exactly the same shares that are held by many other trusts. So as a trust grows, its flexibility declines and, if it has experienced high growth in the past, its performance will tend to fall back to the average of its sector (see Figure 1).

Thus there is a direct conflict of interest between ordinary savers and their fund managers. We would make better returns if our funds remained small and nimble. But managers want to attract as much money as possible to increase their earnings. Moreover, once a trust has accumulated a large amount of investors' money, the priority for managers changes from rapid growth in order to attract new funds to avoiding risk in order to retain savers' money and the huge cash flow this generates in fees. If unit trusts used their growth to decrease their fees as a percentage of their holdings, then investors would at least get some benefit from their funds' growth. However, most trusts keep their fees constant, or even increase them, as they become more popular. So growth is hugely beneficial for the management company, but does nothing for investors. In a perverse way, unit trust investors end up paying for marketing and advertising which will most likely dampen the trust's performance potential and thus damage their investment returns, while enormously increasing the fund's profitability for the fund management company. Possibly more worrying is the fact that most of us place our money in those unit trusts that have just grown rapidly and whose performance is likely to decline as they become too large and ponderous and have just turned into immensely productive cash cows for their managers. This means we are often putting our savings in the wrong unit trusts at the wrong time and are probably not going to get anything near the returns that we assume from the past performance boasted in the unit trust brochures and advertising.

Reason 25

We hope our unit trusts can beat the market

There are probably two main reasons why most of us put our money in unit trusts. Firstly, we believe they hugely simplify investing decisions and investment management for us. Secondly, we hope that our fund manager will have the skill and knowledge or maybe just luck to get more for our savings than we could have got for ourselves. If unit trusts were unable to consistently beat the market, then there would be little justification for the tens of billions they take in fees from us. Instead we'd be better off just buying shares directly in the ten to twenty largest companies in a market and holding on to them as that would give us performance that was reasonably close to the market average without us having to contribute to keeping unit trust managers and directors in the luxury which most seem to consider as their God-given right.

Believe what we say, not what we do

As the unit trust industry is so huge and so gut-wrenchingly profitable, it goes to great lengths to publicise its successes in managing our money. It spends billions each year (of our money) advertising its triumphs and getting journalists to hype the funds the industry wants to promote. Some of the larger firms take big four-colour ads in our newspapers week after week boasting about the success of some fund or other. This can give the impression that they are somehow better at growing our money than their competitors. However, the major unit trust companies have over a hundred funds each, so it would be surprising if one or two of those didn't give reasonable returns. Unfortunately, due to the need for the media to attract unit trust advertising, we seldom see stories about underperforming funds which have given dismal returns year after year and which have reduced savers' money by a half or more

However, the objective statistics on fund performance suggest that the majority of funds do very little for savers, even though they do make their managers and owners extraordinarily wealthy. In any two to three year period, less than forty per cent of funds beat the overall returns from stock markets. Although not that impressive, even these figures need to be handled with care. Poor-performing funds tend to be closed down and merged into better ones and there is a continuous stream of new funds being created which start small and so tend to outperform the market in their first few years as they go for growth. This creates a 'survivors' bias' which makes funds' performance appear better than it actually is. Research done in the US found that the S&P 500 index outperformed almost ninety per cent of mutual funds (unit trusts) over a ten-year period. The situation is similar in the UK. Most savers would have been better off just buying some shares in the top few companies rather putting their money into mutual funds or unit trusts. More worryingly, the worst-performing unit trusts, the ones the fund management companies tend not to mention in their ads and their PR, managed to turn £1,000 into about £300 over the last ten years, but still took healthy fees while incinerating savers' money.

In theory, unit trust managers should be able to beat the market and get us good returns on our savings. After all, that's why we give them our money. Many will have years of experience and they have huge numbers of analysts and other experts to advise them. But there at least three key reasons why most fail to deliver above market-average returns:

1. They are the market

Thirty or forty years ago, unit trusts might only have accounted for less than a quarter of all of share trading. So, by investing with a unit trust, we could benefit from having experienced managers handling our money and trading mainly against inexperienced outsiders. Now unit trusts and other major financial institutions are responsible for over ninety per cent of all share and bond trading activity. Professional investment managers are the market. This means we have many thousands of investment managers all buying from and selling to each other in an attempt to perform better than each other, but taking a slice of our money in fees every time they buy or sell something. The problem may not be that many managers are lazy or stupid or incompetent, though some certainly are, but rather that there are too many talented and well-resourced teams all competing against each other and all generating a massive amount of research, share-trading activity and costs for ordinary savers. But the whole thing is a 'zero sum game' where the more these funds trade against each other, the more likely they are to end up with similar results. On average, the unit trust industry underperforms the market by about three to four per cent a year, which is basically the same as the costs the industry takes for managing our money. Because funds are the market, as a group the best most can ever achieve over three years or more is the market average minus their costs.

2. Their hands are tied

Many of us probably assume that unit trust managers are in a much better position to choose shares than we are. After all, they work full-time in the financial services industry, presumably have a vast amount of knowledge about what's happening and are backed up by teams of analysts and other researchers. However, many fund managers find their hands are tied and they are unable to operate with the same freedom as an ordinary investor. For a start, their performance is usually measured against that of other managers in their sector quarterly or even monthly. This makes it very difficult for them to bet on an original or contrarian position, because if their bet doesn't come good almost immediately, their fund's performance will severely lag behind that of their peers and they will be seen as failing. This tends to result in many managers following broadly similar strategies and buying the same shares. During the dotcom boom, a couple of contrarian managers were fired for underperformance because they refused to jump on the high-tech bandwagon. When the crash came and other funds plummeted down in value, these managers' former funds suddenly became some of the best performers. For many unit trust managers it's safer for their careers to be wrong with the crowd in the short term, rather than be right from betting against the crowd over the longer term.

A second issue is that unit trusts will tend to move en masse in the same direction. Because of their huge buying power, they often push up the prices of the shares or bonds they are targeting to unsustainable levels that are not linked to the financial results of the companies whose shares they are acquiring or the real worth of the bonds. This can create a series of mini-bubbles which then deflate as the unit trust managers move on. Rather than buying at the 'right time', the movement of unit trust money means many managers will buy when shares are overvalued.

A third problem is that many unit trusts are specialised. This leaves them constrained to only invest in specific sectors – emerging markets, green businesses, ethical firms, medium cap companies, high-dividend shares, growth stocks or whatever. At some point, with changing investment tastes and different companies thriving at different stages of the economic cycle, any sector will either come into fashion or become unfashionable. If this happens, we ordinary savers can move our money to somewhere that's more popular and so gives better returns.

Specialised funds don't have this flexibility. They have to remain in their chosen sector. The only flexibility they have is to move their money between shares, bonds and cash to benefit from share price rises and to try to mitigate the effects of share price falls.

3. From hero to zero

Much has been written about the fact that funds, which perform well for a couple of years, often follow that with a period of poor results. One reason is that with new funds, managers focus on achieving rapid growth as this is what will attract new investors. Then when the fund doubles or triples in size, it becomes less flexible and so it is more difficult to repeat previous above-average results (see *Reason 24 – We put our trust in unit trusts*). Sometimes high performance may be purely accidental – a fund may have invested in an area like emerging markets or growth stocks or corporate bonds which becomes the latest investment fad so the shares or bonds it holds rapidly increase in value. Investors lured into funds which have performed well due to their sector becoming the 'in thing' are destined to be disappointed when the big money moves on and that sector slumps back again.

> **"Buying funds purely on their past performance is one of the stupidest things an investor can do."**[31]

Even if you do chance upon a great fund manager who can consistently achieve better results than his or her peers, that may not help you with deciding where to put your money. Many fund managers stay in position about two to three years before moving on to other funds or other fund management companies. So, by the time your star manager has demonstrated two, three or even more years of great returns, it's likely they'll move elsewhere, leaving their unit trust in someone else's hands. Of course, even if a star manager you've spotted moves on, you can decide to follow them and hopefully benefit from their magic touch at whatever fund they find themselves. But few of us have the time or knowledge to know who actually manages the unit trusts we invest in, how well they perform compared to other managers and when they change jobs. So, finding and following the top performers can be more than difficult.

Fund managers and their marketing departments are well aware of the fact that the saving public doesn't realise that today's winners will often turn out to be tomorrow's also-rans. So time and again they use past results and tables ranking fund performance to attract our money. Usually it works.

Do you feel lucky?

Of course, you or I may be well-advised, talented or just lucky and, out of the six thousand or so available funds, we may choose some of the six hundred that consistently can outperform the market average. In this case, we'll get excellent returns on our savings. Moreover, even if ninety per cent of unit trusts under-perform the market average, most should still give us better results than if we kept our money in a bank. But when deciding to put our savings in unit trusts we need to be realistic about what they can achieve for us. In particular, we need to actually take account of the warning that 'past performance is no guide to the future' and remember that excellent past performance may be one of the worst, not one of the best, reasons to invest in a unit trust whose adverts, clever name or fancy brochure has caught our attention, which an obedient personal finance journalist is encouraged to gush over or which a possibly self-serving financial adviser is recommending.

Reason 26

We pay too much for our unit trusts

How much will it cost?

If someone is trying to convince you to put your money in a unit trust and you ask them how much you'll be paying in costs each year, they'll probably tell you that the annual management charge is say 1.3 per cent for a fund buying mainly UK shares. It would be higher at around 1.6 per cent for a trust investing in European shares and 1.8 per cent or more for a global or emerging markets fund. If the person was a bit more clued up or more honest, they might admit that there is a total expense ratio (TER) of 2.3 per cent (again this would be more for a fund investing in foreign markets). But it is unlikely that they would reveal that you could actually end up handing over anywhere from three to five per cent of your money each year to the unit trust company, because then you might do a quick mental calculation and come to the conclusion that, if stock markets tend to give about five to six per cent a year above inflation, paying three to five per cent of your money each year to a unit trust manager would not be a particularly brilliant thing to do.

The main reason for unit trusts' high costs is the greed and profiteering of the trust management companies. However, the behaviour of many ordinary savers is also partly responsible for them paying much more than they should in fees and other costs.

Paying through the nose

A typical unit trust investing in UK shares may have an annual fund management charge of about 1.3 per cent. But this is mainly to cover the cost of managing our money and doesn't include things like administration costs, audit fees and legal expenses. Once these are added, you've got the TER which will probably be around 2.3 per cent. But we're not finished yet. Unit trusts are continually buying and selling shares and bonds. These incur transaction costs which include brokerage fees, bid-offer spreads and stamp duty (in the UK). In the 1970s the average unit trust was turning over its portfolio about once every seven years. Nowadays many are churning their holdings, replacing them every fifteen months or even more frequently.

> **"It's as if mutual-fund managers were studying their stocks just long enough to learn they shouldn't have bought them in the first place, then promptly dumping them and starting all over."**[32]

This has led to a large increase in transaction costs which can reach about 1.3 per cent a year. Finally, most unit trusts will have a bid-offer spread of four to five per cent or more between the higher price at which we buy units and the lower price at which we can sell them. As many of us will switch trusts at least every five years, this can add yet another one per cent to the cost of investing. So once we take the total of the TER, transaction costs and the bid to offer spread, it's not unusual to find we're actually paying up to four per cent or more each year for the pleasure of putting our money in a UK unit trust. This cost may be even higher if we choose a global or emerging markets fund.

If we put money in a £100 million unit trust and the value of the investments bought by that trust were to increase by an outstanding eight per cent to £108 million, the unit trust manager would take around £4.6 million of the increase in value and savers would be left with about £3.4 million (see Figure 1).

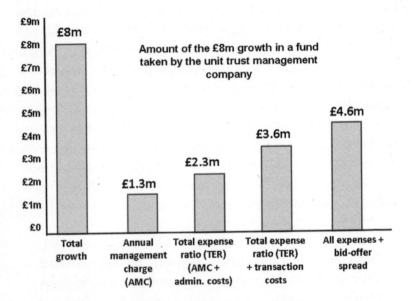

Figure 1 – The fees and charges paid to unit trusts can eat up a large part of any increase in value

If the investments bought by the unit trust were only to achieve a less impressive but more usual five or six per cent growth, then most of this growth would go into the pockets of the trust management company leaving savers on an expensive hiding to nothing.

Competition? What competition?

With the explosive growth in the number of unit trusts and the vast increase in the money they manage, one would have thought that increasing competition and economies of scale would drive down costs. Unfortunately for us, the opposite seems to have happened. In 1980 management fees for equity funds averaged about 0.97 per cent. By 2000 they'd reached 1.50 per cent and now they're around 1.61 per cent. If we just look at the jump from 2000 to 2011, this may seem small at just 0.11 per cent. But with around £500 billion under management in Britain, this tiny almost infinitesimal increase netted fund managers a healthy extra £550 million a year – about £2 million a day. Managers in the US would have got a massive $3.3 billion a year from this seemingly minimal rise in management charges – a much more impressive $13 million a day. Then when you add in perhaps another half a per cent from increased dealing costs as unit trusts buy and sell their holdings ever more frequently, there's another £2.5 billion a year UK savers are losing – £10 million a day – and additional $15 billion a year taken from US mutual funds investors - $58 million a day.

> **"Investors have become victims as the charges they have to pay have risen and risen while the returns they get have been consistently below par and the actual cost of managing their money has continued to fall."**[33]

Market research done by unit trust and mutual funds has shown that not more than one in ten buyers consider costs when deciding which unit trust to choose. The main criteria on which we make our choice is the brand (the fund management company), a choice which is largely influenced by financial advisers, the advertising we've seen and puff pieces written by financial journalists. Next in importance for our selection is the sector – UK companies, emerging markets, commodities funds or whatever. This decision is also usually based on some advice we've been given, article we've read, gossip we've heard or advertising we've seen. Cost seldom plays any role. Knowing that we seem impervious to costs, unit trust companies have realised that they have nothing to lose and everything to gain by remorselessly pushing up their charges even though growth in the amounts of money they manage and advances in computer systems have given them huge efficiency savings which should have brought costs down, but instead have been used to boost their profits.

Still, at least our money is put to good use. Directors of unit trusts typically earn at least twice as much as the directors of the companies whose shares they buy and there are few unit trust managers who are not multimillionaires. As unit trust companies become rich at our expense, there is something we ordinary investors often forget: the fiduciary duty of the directors of unit trust management companies is to maximise profits for their shareholders or owners, not profits for their savers. So, they will try to attract as much savers' money as possible by going for growth in a fund's early years; keep that money for as long as they can by avoiding risk when the fund has a few hundred million under its control; and extract as much of that money as they can for themselves and their shareholders. That's their job.

Our own actions make us poorer

In the 1970s the average unit trust and mutual fund saver held their money in individual trusts for about twelve years. By 2000 this had dropped to three years. Now it may well be even less. Ordinary savers have increasingly treated unit trusts like shares, buying and selling them ever more frequently in the hope of finding one that will be a winner. It's possible to make money jumping from share to share chasing after returns as the cost of buying and selling shares may only be around one per cent or less. But with many unit trusts having a bid-offer spread of up to five per cent, flitting in and out of unit trusts is madness and will have a ruinous effect on our potential returns. Some research has shown that if stock markets return ten per cent in a year (before taking account of inflation), a typical unit trust will achieve around seven per cent, but the average unit trust investor will only get four to five per cent because they are incurring the costs of frequent switching. If the market is only up seven per cent a year, trusts will give about four percent, but the average saver will be lucky to walk away with two per cent. In fact they would have been better off leaving their money in a higher-interest bank savings account. Savers' constant switching makes large amounts of money for financial advisers and fund managers, but can seriously harm most savers' financial health.

But perhaps the worst mistake we make with unit trusts is that we or our financial advisers buy them directly from the companies running them. Many of us buy from the fund management firms because we believe that's the simplest and cheapest way to invest or because we're responding to an ad. Moreover, our financial advisers may encourage us to buy directly from the management companies as that's what gets them the largest commissions. With other products and services, things are usually cheaper if we buy directly from the manufacturer or supplier. But with unit trusts, the exact opposite is true – it's much cheaper to buy them from what's called a 'funds supermarket' rather than directly from the unit trust firms. Normally, we can save five per cent or more by buying from a funds supermarket rather than directly from the management companies. Unit trusts make huge extra profits because many of their investors don't know about funds supermarkets and our financial advisers and the unit trust companies have no interest at all in us finding out much cheaper ways of saving with them.

Reason 27

We underestimate the value of inactivity

Active versus passive?

Within the unit trust and mutual fund industry there is a hot debate about whether savers should invest in actively-managed or index-tracker funds. With actively-managed funds, managers supported by teams of analysts and research staff are supposed to scour the market for shares or bonds which the managers believe will give better returns than the market average. With index-trackers (also called 'passive funds') managers just try to copy the overall performance of an index like the FTSE 100, S&P 500 or MSCI World through either buying all the shares in that index or, for larger markets, buying a sample of the shares. The advantages of active funds are that they can theoretically outperform the market because they can identify the best opportunities and can react to events like a collapse in banking stocks or a rise in the price of energy shares. The disadvantages are that they are expensive and anywhere between seventy and ninety per cent fail to beat the market consistently over a few years. Passive funds benefit investors because, as they don't need expensive management teams, they have low costs and whatever happens to different share types they will give almost the same returns as the overall market. However, in turbulent times when there are bubbles or other shocks in specific sectors, passive funds have no flexibility to react as they must maintain the shares that match the overall make-up of the index they are tracking (see Figure 1).

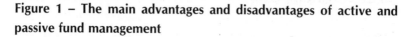

Advantages	Disadvantages
Active: - Can outperform the market - Research-based investing - Flexible reactions to events	**Active:** - High cost - Churn to find winners - Most underperform the market
Passive: - Low cost - No need to monitor performance - Spreads risk across the market	**Passive:** - Get slaughtered in bubbles - Return slightly less than index - No flexibility to react

Figure 1 – The main advantages and disadvantages of active and passive fund management

The traditional model of entrusting money to a fund manager who could pick winning stocks came under attack in the 1970s. Many studies, of which two of the most influential were *Challenge to Judgement* and *The Loser's Game*, suggested that the majority of fund managers underperform the overall market average.[34] In any single year just over half of all so-called 'actively managed' funds outperform the market, with about forty five per cent underperforming it. However, *The Loser's Game* revealed that over the previous decade eighty five per cent of all institutional investors who tried to beat the stock market underperformed the S&P 500 index.

These studies led to the creation of index-tracker funds. The first was launched in the US in 1976, a year after *The Loser's Game* appeared. These have hugely increased in popularity since the early 1990s. By creating an index fund that mirrors the whole market, the inefficiencies and costs of paying experts to select supposedly winning stocks are avoided. Index funds which just track the market often only charge between 0.3 and 0.5 per cent and have much lower transaction costs as they buy and sell much less frequently than active funds. This means that their total costs can be below one per cent. Over the longer term, index trackers have managed to beat most actively managed funds because of their lower costs.

In fact, although they claim to be actively managed, many of the larger actively-managed unit trusts are actually what are called 'closet trackers'. They have so much money that they have to buy most of the main shares in a market and end up just matching the overall market's performance, minus their costs. This leads to savers paying a high price for supposed active management but actually only getting tracker-fund results. If you look at the shares held by some of the larger unit trusts in any country or sector, you'll see the same companies coming up again and again. After all, you could hardly have a European unit trust which didn't buy heavily into companies like Nestlé, Roche, Siemens and Deutsche Bank.

However, not all is happiness and contentment in the world of index trackers. A few of the better known brands have management charges of more than one per cent for almost exactly the same product as we can buy for a third of a per cent.

> **"Some index funds are taking the 'mickey' with high upfront fees and high TERs. Vote with your wallet and avoid them."**[35]

And there are trackers with punitive upfront and back-end costs which their more efficient and less greedy competitors don't even have.

A difficult decision for savers

There is an awful lot at stake here for financial services insiders. As passive funds tend to cost at least two to three per cent less than active funds due to lower management costs and lower levels of trading, a major exodus from active to passive funds could lose financial insiders over $60 billion a year in the US - $235 million a day - and more than £10 billion a year in Britain – about £40 million a day. That's not the kind of money active managers are going to give up without a fight. So they spend several billion of savers' money each year on advertising, marketing and PR and billions more on commissions to salespeople and financial advisers to keep our money pouring into their supposedly actively-managed, but often underperforming, products.

Currently, we ordinary investors only have about ten per cent of our money in passive funds. This is partly because around three quarters of all unit trust investments are made through financial advisers. Active funds pay advisers generous commissions while index trackers pay little or nothing to advisers. This means advisers have a huge vested interest in encouraging their clients to choose active rather than passive trusts. So, passive funds have not yet made a major dent in the incomes of the unit trust management industry. But larger institutional investors have a better understanding of the advantages of passive funds and now have over twenty per cent of their money with index trackers. So it seems that the trend is moving in favour of trackers. In the 1960s and 1970s, investors fled from using stockbrokers because unit trusts provided a much more efficient and effective way of investing. As investment returns remain muted in the new Age of Austerity and costs become more significant to savers, we may be about to enter a new era where only a madman or fool would pay the high costs of active management when similar or better performance can be achieved at a fraction of the cost by using a tracker (see Figure 2).

When receiving an award at a recent investment awards ceremony one active fund manager was quoted as saying, 'I would just like to say thank you to all those index trackers out there who have created the opportunities to be exploited'.[36] In any year, about half of actively-managed funds will beat index trackers. Over three years this falls to about thirty per cent, twenty five per cent over five years and around ten per cent over ten years. It's easy for the small minority of managers who beat tracker funds in any particular year or couple of years to thump their chests in triumph at their own success and be smug about the supposed fools who use trackers. But the majority of us who have money in actively-managed trusts will have our savings tied up for several years, so for us there's only about a one in ten chance of our funds beating trackers. This means that supposedly humorous quips by multimillionaire fund managers about the weaknesses of trackers may not reflect the reality that we ordinary savers have to live with. The almost impossible challenge for us savers is to identify which of the thousands of available funds will be the top performers of the future and thus beat the trackers. If we can't do that, we're wasting most of our potential investment gains by paying high costs for the dismal performance delivered by generously remunerated managers at nine out of ten actively-managed funds.

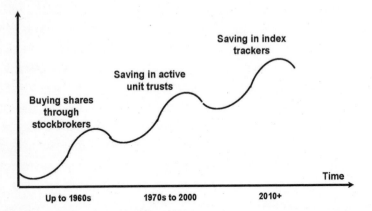

Figure 2 – We may be about to enter an era where the smart money moves out of actively managed unit trusts and into index trackers

There are plenty of conflicting theories about which types of funds perform best in different market conditions. Some people believe that trackers are better in slowly rising markets, whereas active funds perform best in volatile or falling markets. But there are probably just as many experts who have computers full of figures proving exactly the opposite.

Logically, choosing a passive fund should make sense for most savers. However, the fly in the ointment is the fact that stock-market price movements have become increasingly volatile and are possibly often driven by massive market manipulation by insiders rather than reflecting the state of the economy or the underlying value of the shares (see *Reason 23 – Stock markets may be rigged against us*). If this is the case then actively-managed funds may be better placed to spot and take defensive action against or profit from real or artificially-engineered booms and busts in the prices of individual shares or sectors. Passive funds, on the other hand, cannot react.

Reason 28

We fall for the fund of funds fallacy

Once upon a time, unit trusts (mutual funds in the US) were invented to give savers a simple one-stop shop where they could invest their money in stock markets by putting it in the hands of professional fund managers who would hopefully pick the best shares for them. Unit trusts and mutuals were so profitable that financial services companies rushed out thousands of new ones leading to a situation where there are more trusts and funds than there are companies for them to invest in. Now that savers are faced with the problem of how to choose the right unit trusts or mutuals from the many thousands available, the finance industry has come up with a new product – funds of funds (FoFs) also called multi-manager funds (MMFs). These are unit trusts which invest in other unit trusts rather than buying shares or bonds directly themselves. Their main selling point to us savers is that their professional managers will seek out the best unit trust managers and invest our money with them for us.

> **"Possibly one of the biggest scams I have witnessed in my lifetime is the concept of funds of funds."**[37]

The initial idea behind FoFs was sensible. There were many hedge funds and venture capital funds with minimum investment requirements of anything from £25,000 to £100,000 or more. This put them beyond the reach of most ordinary savers. So FoFs were formed to aggregate savers' money and thus get access to these funds with high minimum thresholds. However, as with most financial products, the financial services industry saw the huge profits to be made from their new product and so were soon offering it to people in the mass market who probably didn't have the time, knowledge or experience to understand what they were being sold and how much they were actually going to pay.

The theoretical value to savers of FoFs is that they will weed out the disasters from the many thousands of available unit trusts and find us the gems which will make our money grow. We can get some idea of the amount of detritus in the unit trust industry from the fact that one FoF boss revealed that he quickly screened out eighty five per cent of all funds for inconsistent performance before developing a shortlist to analyse in more detail to choose the ones to invest in. So, if eighty five per cent of all unit trusts are considered by industry insiders to be little more than garbage, then clearly FoFs can have an important role to play in helping us savers put our money in the right place.

> **"The more time you spend as a fund of funds manager, the more you realise there aren't that many good fund managers out there."**[38]

Unfortunately it's quite difficult for us to compare the performance of FoFs. Many have names including wonderfully enticing words like 'income' and 'growth', but which don't tell us if they're straightforward unit trusts or FoFs. Moreover, none of the main funds information sites split FoFs off as a group, so we can't easily see their results.

Pay more, get less?

We've already seen (see *Reason 26 – We pay too much for our unit trusts*) that actively-managed trusts focused on savers' home markets can easily cost at least three per cent a year, with trusts targeting foreign markets charging even more. But when we save in a FoF, we're not only paying the FoF's charges, but we're also covering the charges for the underlying unit trusts in which the FoF has put our money. Up till 2007 many FoFs only listed their charges which tended to be about one per cent and so they looked deceptively cheap compared to most unit trusts and mutual funds. But in 2007 the US Securities and Exchange Commission made FoFs reveal their full fees including the fees of the funds where they invested, what were called 'Acquired Fund Fees and Expenses'. In Britain, most fund ratings firms and websites now include the charges of the FoFs and the underlying funds. So, while the total expense ratio of a typical unit trust might be anywhere from 1.6 to 2.5 per cent, many FoFs have charges of somewhere between 2.3 and 3.2 per cent.

In the thirty boom years from 1977 to 2007, when savers could expect double-digit returns and when FoFs started to take off, anything up to an extra one per cent paid to a FoF manager to find the best unit trusts was probably a worthwhile expense for savers. But if real returns over the next five to ten years are going to be nearer the long-term average of five per cent after taking inflation into account, the extra cost of a FoF seems difficult to justify.

The most expensive tracker on the market?

FoFs should reduce risk for savers. Instead of finding they've chosen one of the eighty five per cent of funds which one FoF manager considers are unreliable or even dead losses, the FoF should spread our money across several better-managed trusts thus preventing us getting wiped out by one or two poor managers were we to choose our unit trusts ourselves. However, suppose a FoF puts our money into thirty different unit trusts and suppose each of those holds on average shares in fifty companies, then our money will be in 1,500 companies. Actually, it will be in slightly fewer as there will be some overlap – several of the unit trusts bought by the FoF will have invested in the same shares. But the problem here is that once your savings are spread across so many shares through a FoF, you're almost so diversified that you might as well just buy an index tracker fund for a fraction of the cost rather than paying two levels of charges to a FoF. So there is a very fine dividing line between what you'll get from many FoFs and what simple tracker funds will give you at about a tenth of the cost.

Moreover, FoFs are much less flexible than most unit trusts. A FoF can't react if bank shares collapse or pharma shares shoot up. All it can do is hope the unit trusts holding our money do react. Of course, it can sell some unit trusts if those trusts don't react effectively to market movements, but by then it's usually a bit late and the gains have been missed or the losses already made.

The dangers of incest

A further difficulty with FoFs is that, however independent they may claim to be, many just shove our money into unit trusts run by the companies that own the FoFs. Some may be open about this and specify that they just invest in their organisation's unit trusts. Others may have a home bias, so they do put money into other companies' funds, but tend to be overweight in products run by their owners. Too often with FoFs, we're not really getting a true FoF, all they're doing is funnelling part or all of our savings into their owners' products.

Why not D.I.Y?

FoFs clearly offer a great deal of reassurance to cautious or time-constrained savers overwhelmed by the choice of thousands of trusts and funds. And up to one per cent extra in fees to a FoF manager may seem like a small price to pay for an experienced financial services insider to select the best funds for us. However, of all the available investment services, FoFs are probably the one that is easiest for us to do ourselves. We can't rely on our financial adviser or bank to recommend a unit trust for us as they'll be too influenced by their narrow experience and by commission rates. But we can get some of the FoFs managers' hard work screening unit trusts absolutely free. All we need to do is email the best few FoF management companies requesting information about investing with them. In all their blurbs we'll find a list of the main unit trusts they invest in. So we could just choose a few of those recommended unit trusts for our savings and, of course, buy them direct from a funds supermarket. At least we'll know that some experienced FoF managers have interviewed the unit trust management teams and have confidence in them. That's not a bad start for us in the struggle to sort out the ten to fifteen per cent of good unit trusts from the eighty five to ninety per cent we shouldn't touch with even a well-insulated barge pole.

Reason 29

We want a slice of hedge fund magic

Here they come

Most of us probably never thought we'd ever have to worry about hedge funds taking some of our money. For the majority of people, hedge funds are probably seen as exotic ways for the mega-rich to invest that few of us really understand. The only time we hear about them is when a big one goes spectacularly bust or when self-serving politicians refuse to accept that collapsing stock markets, falling currencies and financial turmoil are the results of their overspending and incompetent economic management and so they try to find a scapegoat like supposedly evil speculators and sinister hedge-fund managers to blame for the mess the politicians have caused.

But hedge funds are going to affect ever more of us. For a start, many pension funds are putting increasing quantities of our savings into the, sometimes not very trustworthy but always highly paid, hands of hedge-fund managers. And secondly, hedge funds are out to convince more of us to entrust them with our money. So we will increasingly find financial advisers, journalists and other financial products sellers eagerly encouraging us to consider including hedge funds as part of our savings portfolios. As fore-warned is fore-armed, I'd like to just touch on what hedge funds can do both for us and to us.

Winning on the ups and the downs

In the investment world, 'going long' on something is when we invest in the hope of a price rise, 'going-short' means benefiting if the price falls. Almost all the investments we normally buy are what is called 'long-only'. This means we can only get a positive return if the price goes up and we are able to sell them for more than we bought them. Whether we put our savings in unit trusts, gold, pension funds, property, ostriches, vintage cars, fine wines, stamps or whatever, rising prices are usually good for us and falling prices not quite so desirable.

Hedge funds can go long or short on a huge variety of investments including shares, derivatives, options and different types of sophisticated securities. So, providing the hedge-fund manager makes the right bet, unlike most other investments, hedge funds can make massive amounts of money in both rising and falling markets. In the 1980s and 1990s, returns from the stock market were so high that hedge funds had limited attractions for most investors. However, more recently we've had what has been called 'the lost decade' as any money put into stock markets in 2000 is probably worth the same or even less than when it was originally invested. Faced with appallingly low interest rates, ten years of dismal stock-market performance and the likelihood of five to ten more years of economic stagnation (see *Reason 18 – We think stock markets will always rise*) savers are looking for something that will give reasonable returns. With their potential to make money whatever the market conditions, hedge funds may seem to be a perfect solution for investors who need better returns than long-only investments will be able to deliver if stock markets remain fairly stagnant for the next five or more years.

Getting mom and pop's money

Originally hedge funds tended to attract money from a few super-rich individuals who could afford to put in six- and seven-figure sums. But faced with poor returns from stock markets and fixed-interest savings, many big life insurance companies and pension funds have been moving some of our money out of shares and bonds into hedge funds in the hope of better results. We can't usually invest directly in hedge funds as few of us have the minimum amounts required and because financial regulators consider hedge funds too complex and risky to allow them to solicit money directly from ordinary people. However, hedge funds have succeeded in lobbying financial regulators to allow us ordinary savers, what they call 'retail investors', to invest in hedge funds through hedge fund funds of funds (FoFs) – that is unit trusts and mutual funds which put our money into what they consider to be the best hedge funds.

"Retail investors will be free to plough their cash into funds of hedge funds after the City watchdog (the Financial Services Authority) said yesterday that 'mom and pop' savers should have wider access to alternative assets."[39]

We may be told by financial products sellers that being 'allowed' to put our money into hedge funds represents a great opportunity, previously only available to the super-wealthy. But we should always exercise a great deal of caution when financial services insiders seem to be doing us ordinary savers a favour.

Selling the incomprehensible to the uncomprehending?

The financial services industry has a long and fairly shameful history of developing quite sophisticated (and usually immensely profitable) financial products which suit a small niche group of customers and then rushing off to flog these to the mass market where many buyers probably have little understanding of the complexities of what they are buying and the risks they are running. Most often the mass-marketing of financial products is driven by the straightforward urge to make as much money as possible. Though sometimes, as with the case of Lloyds insurance market, the panic to draw in money from less well-informed savers could appear to be little short of deliberate massive fraud. In the 1970s, the Lloyds insurance market was faced with catastrophic losses, mainly due to asbestos-related claims in the US. Quickly this once elite institution, whose members were all supposedly honourable people from the top echelons of society, embarked on a massive and cynical recruitment drive to encourage thousands of people to sign up as 'names' largely by appealing to their snobbery and greed. At the time the financial press was effusive about this great, once-in-a-lifetime opportunity for some lucky people to join one of the world's most exclusive groups of investors. But the new names were seemingly being recruited for a very specific purpose. Most were shoved into the syndicates with the greatest exposure to losses and many lost their shirts and more as Lloyds names have unlimited liability. There were even a few suicides. By offering outsiders a supposed 'investment opportunity', Lloyds insiders got the suckers to generously pay most of the losses and the original ever so honourable Lloyds members emerged with their finances gloriously intact.

With hedge funds offering us the 'opportunity' to invest with them, some commentators have suggested that original investors are wising up to the risks of hedge-fund investing and pulling out. As one writer explained, 'Now that hedge funds are seeing enormous withdrawals of capital by their investors and now that something like half the hedge funds in the world will face dissolution, people are beginning to understand the real risks hedge funds faced.'[40] So like Lloyds members and other groups of financial services insiders when faced with potential losses, perhaps hedge fund managers are worrying about their own financial futures and so are casting around for the next group of fools to fleece. That's where we ordinary savers come, usually naively, into the picture.

Beware the 'fat tail'

Hedge funds are generally associated with either making massive profits or going horrifically belly up. In fact, hedge fund performance has been fairly prosaic and not quite as exciting as the financial press would often have us believe. In the big share boom years of 1980 to 2000, the S&P 500 index beat hedge funds by around six per cent a year. However, in the 'lost decade' from 2000 to 2010, the situation was reversed with hedge funds outperforming shares by about six or seven per cent a year. The indications are that in a raging bull market with share prices shooting relentlessly up, most index tracker funds will do better than hedge funds, whereas in falling or stagnant markets, being able to go long or short enables hedge funds to deliver better results than most other investment types.

But as financial advisers and journalists come touting hedge funds by showing us how well hedge funds have performed in the past, we have to be very careful. It's estimated that about one in every seven hedge funds collapses every year. In some years, the failure rate has reached one in five. Just in the first three months of 2010 around two hundred and forty hedge funds were liquidated. This makes indexes of hedge fund performance highly misleading due to the 'survivors' bias' – they only measure the performance of the funds which continue to operate and almost pretend that the many embarrassing failures, however huge and costly, never existed.

Investments like unit trusts can only lose some or all of the money we put into them. In fact, although some have succeeded in losing two thirds of savers' money, few have ever actually gone bust. However, hedge funds can leverage their money to gamble at least ten times the amount invested in them. If a few of their bets go wrong, the losses can be horrendous. The most famous hedge-fund bust in history was Long-Term Capital Management which managed to turn $1 billion of investors' money into almost $4 billion of losses and almost brought down the world's financial system in the process. But there have been several other catastrophes which vaporised billions of investors' money yet allowed their managers to walk away from the smoking rubble with hundreds of millions of investors' money safely ensconced in their own bank accounts. Many hedge funds will make respectable returns, but the industry has what is called a 'fat tail' – a small group of funds that can lose eye-watering amounts of investors' money while still making their managers rich beyond most people's wildest imagination.

This is how to make money

Hedge funds tend to charge more than most of the other investments we will be offered. This is perhaps understandable given the complexity of the investments they make. Typically they work according to what's called a '2 and 20'. They take two percent of investors' money each year in management fees and then twenty per cent of any gains they make as a performance bonus. With around £1.8 trillion invested in hedge funds globally, hedge fund managers are taking an awful lot of investors' money. If we assume annual growth of nine per cent (six per cent real growth plus three per cent due to inflation) hedge funds will earn their managers about £36 billion a year in management costs and another £32 billion in performance fees. Even a relatively small hedge fund with say £3 billion under management will net its managers over £100 million a year. As there may only be ten to twenty people involved in running such a fund, there's quite a lot of money to go round in great, big, fat, juicy salaries and bonuses.

In addition, the FoFs which want our money to put into hedge funds also have charges. Usually these range from '1 and 10' to '1 and 20' – one per cent in management fees and anything from ten to twenty per cent of the profits. These FoF management and performance fees can also take quite a chunk of savers' cash. For example, if a hedge fund FoF goes up by a very respectable ten per cent in a year, we would pay around six per cent in charges and only be left with four per cent or less. In fact, due to their high charges a hedge fund FoF would need to grow by closer to fifteen per cent a year for ordinary savers' money to beat the overall long-term performance of the main stock-market indices. That's quite a stretch. However, if stock markets are going to be stagnant or falling for the next five or ten years, then hedge fund FoFs might give us much better returns, in spite of their high costs. So we cannot dismiss them altogether.

It seems that hedge fund FoFs have been struggling over the last couple of years with the number closing exceeding the number of new launches. They are also being threatened by new European Union legislation. But they remain popular in the US where they are able to operate with less regulation. It's likely that some of our money will find its way into hedge fund FoFs, either directly from financial advisers convincing us to put cash into them or through our pension fund managers using them as a way of trying to improve their returns in the dismal market conditions we're likely to have for the next five or more years. Whether we will get any benefits from this is, like with all investments, questionable. The only thing which is absolutely certain with hedge fund FoFs is that both hedge-fund and FoF managers will become extraordinarily wealthy while the majority of people with money in hedge-fund FoFs will not understand what they are buying or has been bought for them, the real charges they are paying and the risks they are running.

Reason 30

We think 'with profits' means profits for us

In the Hall of Fame for Financial Horrors, with-profits products deserve a special place of honour in view of the amount of money they have made for financial services insiders while delivering abjectly disappointing returns for most of the people who knowingly or unwittingly have money invested in them. About ten million of us have around £400 billion in almost seventeen million with-profits products. These can be pensions, endowment mortgages, life insurance policies or with-profits bonds. There was a big boom in sales of with-profits products in the 1990s and early 2000s with up to £15 billion a year going into them. In the last few years they've only attracted about £3 billion a year, but in spite of their generally dreadful performance they continue to be sold.

"There are some people who reckon there is nothing inherently wrong with with-profits but the numbers of people who disagree will outweigh them by a country mile."[41]

Too smooth, by half

With-profits savings schemes were sold mainly to cautious investors who were looking for better returns than they could get from a bank account without being exposed to too much stock-market risk. They were seen as a safe way to save for things like school fees or retirement. With-profits differ from other investments because they claim that they 'smooth' returns for investors. With most investments, an investor gets the value of the underlying investment after the investment management company has taken its costs, fees and bonus payments. With with-profits, the manager smoothes the returns for investors by holding back some of the returns in good years so there is money to pay out something to investors even if the value of the underlying investments is stagnant or falls in poor years. Unfortunately, when being sold these products many savers may have got the wrong impression from the salesperson, intentionally or otherwise, that with-profits products somehow reduced risk and guaranteed profits. But they don't. If the shares bought for a with-profits product fall in value, then the value of people's savings will also fall.

Heads I win: tails you lose?

There have been many problems with the structure of these products which have led to them being immensely profitable for financial services providers and miserably disappointing for all but a handful of savers:

- **High commission rates** – with-profits were very attractive to financial advisers and other sellers as they paid opening commissions of up to seven per cent. This was considerably more than the three per cent paid by most unit trusts and the zero per cent paid by almost all index-tracker funds. Given that the average with-profits fund is worth around £30,000, this gave the seller up to £2,100 for signing someone up whereas a unit trust would only have paid them around £900. Cynics might feel that the enthusiasm with which many financial advisers promoted with-profits had more to do with the generous levels of commission than whether the products would make savers quite as rich as the sales spiel suggested.

- **High costs** – typical annual management charges for with-profits tend to be at least four per cent. With average stock-market returns running at between five and six per cent, handing four per cent a year to the management company would clearly eat into the potential profits savers might make.

- **Poor returns** – each year the managers and actuaries of with-profits products have to make a decision about how to spend any gains. They can either hold on to profits in case performance the next year isn't so good; take the money for themselves in bigger salaries and bonuses; pass the money on to their shareholders in the form of dividends; or give the money back to investors. Being cautious people, actuaries tend to retain as much of the profits as they think they can get away with. So you often find that a good portion of any profits are retained for future, possibly poorer years rather than being doled out to savers. As for the money that is actually paid out, it often seems that a strict pecking order is applied. 'Charity begins at home' means that first bite goes to investment managers in salary increases and bonuses. Next in line come shareholders as executives of with-profits management companies have a fiduciary duty to maximise profits for their shareholders, not investors. Finally any crumbs are distributed back to investors. In one year, for example, one of the largest with-profits fund management companies issued a press release boasting that their with-profits had 'delivered strong per-formance', presumably beating their own drum to attract more savers' money. In spite of this apparently admirable 'strong performance', payouts to investors were cut by seventeen per cent yet the management company made record profits and paid its staff eye-watering bonuses.

- **Keeping back surpluses** – because they hold back so much money, over time many with-profits accumulate healthy surpluses, well in excess of what is needed to pay managers, shareholders and savers. This money is called 'inherited estate'. The financial regulator has insisted that ninety per cent of this inherited estate should be returned to savers. But managers have found many ingenious ways of getting around this and instead have used much of this money for their own benefit by paying tax on dividends given to their shareholders and paying fines for mis-selling. One of the major companies, for example used £1.6 billion of its £8.7 billion inherited estate to pay fines and compensation for mis-selling. So, costs that should have been borne by executives and shareholders were instead paid by savers. Another trick companies try is what's called 'reattribution' – they offer a part of the inherited estate back to savers in return for savers agreeing to give up their rights to the rest. Another of the larger management groups with £2.4 billion in inherited estate wrote to their savers proposing that they accept just £1 billion to be paid out over three years rather than wait longer for a possibly higher payment. Not knowing any better, the majority of savers accepted this less than generous offer. The managers and shareholders then pocketed the remaining £1.4 billion when they should have taken just £240 million and actually given savers £2.16 billion – a pretty smart and apparently legal way to snaffle over a billion pounds of savers' money. Naturally the main financial services regulator saw nothing, heard nothing, said nothing and did nothing.

- **Beware of zombies** – due to their poor performance and consistently bad press, with-profits schemes have become less popular and more than half are now closed to new investors. Managers of these so-called 'zombie funds' no longer have much incentive to achieve stunning investment performance as they are not interested in attracting new investment. So they tend cut their costs down to a minimum and to shove most of the money they manage into simple, low-return, stable investments like government bonds. This enables them to use the funds as cash-cows – giving high profits to managers for very little work. Sometimes with-profits firms just get rid of their zombie funds – about £110 billion of zombie funds have been sold to other companies who just milk them for their management fees without worrying unduly about returns for savers. This was described by one financial website, 'The only people making money out of closed with-profits funds are the vulture companies who bought them and are creaming off massive management fees.'[42]

Trapped

Given their poor performance, high costs and history of fleecing savers, you might have thought that most people with with-profits would be taking their money out and running for the hills. Unfortunately, this is often quite difficult. Many with-profits companies have imposed what they sometimes optimistically call 'Market Value Adjusters' (MVAs) and sometimes more honestly call 'Market Value Reductions' (MVRs). These are penalties of anything between ten to twenty five per cent of savers' money taken by the fund manager in the case of an early withdrawal. For example, of the £78,719 that I have in a NPI with-profits pension policy set up by a previous employer, I would lose £10,927 in MVA if I tried moving my money to another pension manager in order to avoid NPI's high annual management charges and disappointing investment performance. That makes escaping NPI's unloving embrace a fairly costly exercise for me. Some with-profits contracts do have an escape clause allowing savers to withdraw their money without penalties ten or fifteen years after they started saving. However, this clause is often hidden deep within the contractual terms and conditions, so many people don't know they have this option. Moreover, the period for withdrawing money may be as short as one day, so the slightest delay can result in large losses for savers.

"In summary, my advice would be to steer well clear of with-profits funds of all shapes and varieties. Although they appeared to work in the good times, they are very much 'yesterday's products' and have little to offer to today's investors."[43]

With financial products, the greater the complexity of the investments, the more profitable they are for the sellers and managers and the more financially damaging they tend to be for savers. There are a small minority of with-profits products which have given good returns. But for most savers, their experience with with-profits has been decidedly without-profits and in too many cases has yielded painful results.

Reason 31

We try our hand at spread betting

We're increasingly seeing advertising for spread betting in investing and money management publications. In the one I subscribe to, four or five different spread betting companies take full-page colour ads each week, outnumbering any other type of advertising. Spread betting ads are already common in the business sections of many weekend newspapers and will probably soon start to appear in the personal finance sections. Spread betting could appear deceptively attractive to many savers. After all, money in a bank, shares or unit trusts will at best give us about a miserable five per cent a year before tax. Yet a reasonable run on spread betting can easily let you pocket ten per cent a week – five hundred per cent a year – completely and gloriously tax-free. So spread betting can let you earn in just one year what it would take a hundred years or more to achieve with most other investments.

Spread betters gamble on price movements of anything from individual shares, currencies and commodities to whole markets like the FTSE, Dax or S&P. It is called spread betting because the company providing the service makes most of their money by putting an additional spread around the price at which something is being bought or sold.

Spread betting appears to have many advantages compared to traditional investing:

- **You don't have to buy anything** – It allows you to bet on price movements without having to buy the underlying assets – shares, commodities or foreign exchange.

- **It's tax-free** – When you buy or sell shares, get paid dividends or receive interest from a bank you will have to pay taxes like stamp duty, capital gains and income tax. Unless spread betting is your full-time job and only source of income, there are no taxes to be paid as it's considered to be gambling.

- **You can go long or short** – When you spread bet you can gain just as much whether prices rise or fall, providing you guess the direction correctly. With most other investments, you need the price to go up before you make a profit.

- **You can bet on a rise or fall at the same time** – If the FTSE, for example, is trading at 5551-5552, you can place two bets, one that it will rise and one that it will fall. These only get triggered when the FTSE actually moves. So if it starts going up, your bet that it will rise gets triggered. Similarly if it drops, only your bet that it will fall is triggered. So it can seem that, come rain or shine, you'll probably win.

- **Huge leverage** – If you bet say £50 a pip (a pip is usually the minimum price movement you can bet on), you can easily win four or five times your original bet if the price moves in the right direction. On a really good bet, you can win much much more.

- **You can wait for the breakout** – Prices on many shares, currencies, commodities and other things people bet on tend to experience periods of stability followed by bursts of movement up or down, what spread-betters call 'the breakout'. You can place a bet that is only activated when the breakout comes.

- **Loss limits** – You can put conditions in your bet that prevent your losses exceeding your chosen level should

your bet happen to be wrong.
- **You can adjust mid-flight** – With most bets, such as
  with horse racing or on roulette, once the race has started
  or the croupier has called 'no more bets' you have to wait
  helplessly for the result to see if you've won or not. With
  spread betting you can choose to close your bet at any time.
  So if you're ahead, you can take your winnings; if you're
  behind you can either cut your losses or wait in the hope
  that things will change and you'll be up again.

Given all these properties of spread betting, it should be pretty easy
to make a fair bit of money without too much effort. If only.

Gone in a flash

As I write this, I'm nursing a bit of a sore head and an empty wallet.
In the last four weeks I've lost almost £30,000 spread betting for
about an hour a day five days a week. So I managed to blow around
£1,500 an hour. That's really quite a chunk of cash. I'd have to write
five to ten books to earn that money back. Actually, it's not quite as
bad as it looks. Fortunately, I was betting using a few spread-betting
companies' demo sites. These are simulations of their live betting
sites that allow you to practice before you start betting with real
money. I realise that I am no financial genius otherwise I would have
been rich long ago. However, the fact that I managed to squander so
much money so quickly does pose the question - if spread betting
seems so easy, why do so many people get completely wiped out
extremely quickly?

Industry estimates suggest that around ninety per cent of spread-
betters lose most or all of their money and close their accounts
within three months of starting. There seem to be another eight per
cent or so who make reasonable amounts of money on a regular basis
and there are around two per cent of spread-betters who make
fortunes. I've been to a few presentations run by spread betting

companies and at one of these the salesman let slip that over eighty per cent of his customers lost money. Even many professionals lose on about six bets out of every ten. But by controlling their losses and maximising their returns when they win, they can increase their wealth.

Why it can go horribly wrong

There seem to be several reasons why spread betting is so effective at dramatically demolishing most practitioners' wealth:

- **The companies want you to lose** – When you first open a demo or real account, you will get several phone calls from extremely friendly and helpful young men and women at the spread-betting company asking if there's anything they can do to assist you to get going. This is customer service at its very best. Most of the people contacting you will parrot the line that they just want to help and that they're happy if you're successful as their company only makes money from the spread. Some will reassure you that they want you to win as the more you win, the more you're likely to bet and the more the spread-betting company will earn. This may make you feel good, convince you that the company is open, honest, trustworthy and supportive and encourage you to use them for your betting. But it's also a lie. It's true that the company might make a lot of its money from the spread. However, with many of your bets, you're betting against the company and so they hope you lose, big time. In fact, during the last month I've seen several companies change the conditions on their sites to make it more likely that people using them will lose. So, lesson one – spread betting companies are not your friends. The more you lose the more they win. It's that simple.

- **It's difficult to break even** – If you bet say £50 a pip and the price does go the way you want, the spread betting company takes the first £50 you win. So the price has to move two pips in the right direction for you to win your £50 back and three pips for you to emerge with £100, doubling your money. But if the price moves three pips in the wrong direction, you lose your original bet plus £50 a pip, giving a total loss of £200, a loss of four times your original bet.

- **Losses can be massive** – With most gambling, you can only lose what you put down on a horse, blackjack or roulette. With spread betting you can quickly say goodbye to much more than you wager. I forgot to put a stop loss on one bet and managed to lose over £800 with just one £50 bet. Because your bet is leveraged, you can make both fabulous gains and excruciatingly painful losses. Too often it's the latter. The small size of many bets, often £5 or £10 a pip can lull betters into a false sense of security. It's only when the losses go five to ten times the original bet that they realise the risk they have taken.

"The spread betting leverage means that you can get rich which is a wonderfully appealing idea, but it also means you can get poor which most people ignore."[44]

- **You can waste thousands on courses and systems** – At one free spread-betting seminar I attended we were more than strongly encouraged to sign up for a two-day weekend course teaching us how to spread bet successfully. This would normally cost (we were told) £6,995, but there was a special offer for the first five people to sign up of only £1,997. There are many such courses and also gurus offering to sell you their special spread-betting systems, guides, webinars and all sorts of other advice.

With so many supposed experts apparently making a living teaching others how to spread bet, there must be a lot of takers. But I've found that all you need to know and more is available free on the Internet. As one specialist said, 'Don't bother wasting your money on 'Guru' books written by so-called experts. Those books are crap and not worth the paper they are printed on. Nobody sells a secret trading methodology if they are really successful. The only reason these guys are writing books is because they didn't make it as traders'.[45]

- **It's the bobbing about that beats you** – We often hear on the news that the price of gold has risen by a few dollars an ounce or the FTSE has fallen by a hundred and thirty points or that the pound has risen by two cents against the dollar. These reports make price changes on financial instruments sound like smooth movements either up or down. However, the prices of shares, stock markets, commodities and currencies seldom move in straight lines. They jump about every few seconds. So, if the FTSE is at 5540 and you correctly bet £50 a pip that it will go up to 5545 you might not necessarily win £200. In between going from 5540 to 5545, it might drop down a couple of times to say 5535 or lower. If you have a stop loss on at 5536 or 5535 to avoid losing too much money, your stop loss will kick in and you'll lose £250 or £300 even if the index did subsequently move upwards as you predicted. I've placed over a hundred bets to test whether I won when my bets were right. On about eighty per cent I lost in spite of being right because the fluctuations triggered the stop losses even though the index did actually move from where it was to where I predicted it would go. This creates a rather odd situation where stop losses can unfortunately make you lose even when you should be winning. Yet if you don't put stop losses on and things go in the wrong direction, your losses can annihilate you.

- **It attracts losers** – At the spread betting seminars I've attended, I've been shocked by the number of low-paid workers – waiters, porters, kitchen staff, healthcare assistants and impoverished, would-be writers like myself – who decide to have a go at spread betting as they believe that, apart from winning the Lottery, it may be the only realistic way they have of making any money. These people will be betting with their meagre life savings against extremely sophisticated financial services insiders with vast knowledge, many years experience and extraordinarily deep pockets. It's not difficult to guess who is going to win.

Sucker or smartie?

Spread betting is a 'zero sum game'. Unlike depositing our money in a bank so it can be lent to businesses or house-buyers, spread betting doesn't create wealth. It just redistributes money from the suckers to the smart. When contemplating whether to try your hand at spread betting, you need to work out whether you are likely to be in the ninety per cent who end up as suckers or the ten per cent who make money by being smart. I found it interesting that not a single one of the amiable young men and women from spread-betting companies that I spoke to actually did any spread betting themselves. However, if you do manage to spread bet successfully, please drop me an email, I'd love to find out how to do it.

Reason 32

We imagine company bosses care about shareholders' interests

Shares and the dividends they pay look like the best place for us to put our savings if we want to get a return that consistently beats inflation. Anyway, most of us have some of our money in shares, either directly because we've bought some or indirectly through unit trusts and pension savings. The value of our shares depends on the executives and directors of the companies, whose shares we own, fulfilling their fiduciary duty to promote the success of the company for the good of the shareholders. But far too frequently we see company bosses almost hijacking even major organisations and using them to serve their own interests rather than those of shareholders. The result can be executives, their bankers and their advisers walking away from the carnage of their mismanagement with their tens or hundreds of millions intact while our savings either fall in value or are even completely wiped out.

Money, money, money

The most obvious sign of executives being rather more interested in their own rather than their shareholders' bank balances is the extraordinary rise in executive pay compared to what the rest of us could ever hope to earn. In the US in the early 1980s, average chief executive officer pay was about forty times that of the average production worker. By 1990 it was over a hundred times higher. By 2000 it had shot up to three hundred times. By 2004 it was four hundred and thirty times. Today it is over five hundred times.

Bosses' pay packets in the US tend to be the highest in the world. However we've seen a similar explosion in directors' remuneration in Britain. In the ten years from 2000 to 2010 executives at Britain's top one hundred companies managed to increase their take-home earnings by four hundred per cent while ordinary workers got just thirty per cent more. Yet in spite of British executives quadrupling their pay packets over the last decade, anyone buying shares in their companies in 2000 would find that ten years later their investments were worth pretty much the same as they originally paid. In 2010 there were investor protests against possibly excessive executive salaries at several of our best-known companies including Tesco, HSBC and M&S. All these were, of course, in vain as companies shrugged off shareholder anger and justified giving massive pay increases, sometimes to bosses who had overseen impressive losses, by claiming they needed to pay so much to attract the necessary talent.

One of the most entertaining cases in 2010 was probably at BP. In March 2010 BP had to defend paying chief executive Tony Hayward a forty one per cent rise in his pay package from £2.85 million to £4.01 million in spite of a forty five per cent drop in profits.[46] BP claimed that the pay rise was a reward 'for boosting operational performance', seemingly overlooking the inconvenient fact of the collapse in the firm's profitability. BP's chairman and several other senior executives also shared in the large salary increase bonanza. So it must have been cheers and smiles and trebles all round in the BP boardroom. But critics of BP had been concerned for years that BP was taking huge risks with safety by using excessive cost-cutting and reportedly corner-cutting in their attempts to improve the company's financial performance and their own remuneration. There had been several worrying incidents. An explosion at a BP refinery in Texas in 2005 killed fifteen workers, injured over 170 more and cost BP more than £1 billion in compensation and fines. Repeated problems and spills at an Alaskan pipeline fifty one per cent owned by BP also attracted US politicians' attention. The chairman of the House Energy Subcommittee commented, 'My review of the mountain of circumstantial evidence can only lead me to the conclusion that severe pressure for cost-cutting did have an impact on maintenance of pipelines'.[47] Then in April 2010 came the big one – the Gulf of Mexico oil rig explosion killing eleven, injuring twelve and possibly costing BP's shareholders up to $20 billion. Naturally BP's executives mostly kept their jobs and their big pay packets while, if a couple do eventually leave, they will live the rest of their lives in the kind of opulent financial security that anyone with savings or pensions in BP shares is unlikely to ever experience.

Larger companies have remuneration committees which should supposedly be independent of executives and should represent the interests of shareholders. However, most are made up of executives from other companies, executives' cronies, friends, greedy politicians, politicians' wives and various other supposed 'worthies' who make a more than comfortable living sitting on committees where they do as they're told to keep their lucrative positions. This means that too many remuneration committees have a vested interest in continually inflating executives' salaries and doing favours which they hope will be returned. As for the interests of shareholders, forget it – they don't figure in the salary and bonus feeding frenzy going on in many boardrooms across the world.

Fun fiddling the figures

The most common way for executives to boost their earnings is from bonuses and share options. Frequently, as appears to be the case at BP, massive bonuses are justified by executives apparently hitting their performance targets even when profits may be derisory, stagnant or collapsing. In many cases shareholders are not even told what these mysterious targets are. So they suffer the indignity of the value of their investments remaining static or falling, yet see delightedly grinning bosses eagerly stuffing millions of shareholders' money into their own already healthy bank accounts.

However, when executives' remuneration is actually directly linked to increasing shareholder value, executives (also known as 'executhieves') have many ingenious ways of ensuring share prices hit the levels required for them to get their hands on the maximum amount of loot they can. By doing things like moving expenditure or earnings between financial years or changing the way depreciation is calculated, company accounts can be manipulated to give almost any result the bosses want. Studies have also shown that many executives play around with the numbers reducing quarterly results to drive their share prices down just before their share options are granted. This allows them to get them at a nice low price. Then they push gains into their full-year results and sell their options as soon as the shares leap up again when the 'surprisingly better' full-year results are released.

One possibly dubious technique that we savers should watch out for is when a company's management decides to buy back some of its own shares. By reducing the number of shares in circulation, share buybacks usually push up the price of each share that's left in the market. Executhieves try to justify buybacks by claiming they increase shareholder value. But often this isn't true. Firstly, a buyback only increases shareholder value if the shareholder decides to sell at the higher price. People who hold on to their shares for the longer term can find that buybacks reduce shareholder returns - by pushing up the price of shares, buybacks may actually reduce the dividends as a per cent of each share's price. It would usually be better for shareholders if companies just used their extra cash to pay larger dividends to shareholders. However, when top managers are eager to hit a particular share price to get their bonuses, and their dismal performance leads to the share price languishing disappointingly far below the necessary level, buybacks can be an almost magical solution allowing them to get richer at the expense of ordinary savers.

The joys of merger-mania

A further way executhieves can vastly increase their wealth while often reducing the value of shareholders' money is through ill-conceived, badly-planned and poorly-implemented mergers and acquisitions (M&As). Studies have repeatedly shown that only about a third of M&As actually increase shareholder wealth. A further forty per cent have a neutral effect and thirty per cent significantly reduce value for shareholders. Moreover, only one takeover in ten achieves the targets originally cited by top management. Yet the wonderful thing about M&As is that almost a hundred per cent of them result in a large increase in top managers' pay packets.

Part of the problem is that bringing together two organisations can be a lot more difficult and more costly than managers originally anticipated – key people leave, big customers go to competitors, customer service and quality declines as people worry about their job security and internal power struggles reduce competitive strength. However, a greater problem may be that many mergers and acquisitions were never intended to create value for ordinary shareholders in the first place. Instead, they were caused by managers or their advisers seeing opportunities for self-enrichment and/or self-advancement.

The driving force behind many M&As is speculative activity by investment banks. They see opportunities for tens or hundreds of millions of pounds, dollars or euros in fees by encouraging executives at one company to buy or merge with another company. Advisers can show all kinds of convincing numbers about how profits will increase due to the merger or else they can just appeal to executives' egos with promises about how much better an acquired company will perform under their unique brilliant management. The banks don't care about longer-term value for shareholders. Also, they more than anyone understand that seventy per cent of M&As won't actually deliver any value for the shareholders, unit trusts and pension funds with investments in the company doing the acquiring. But that's not their problem. They're after the short-term fees.

> **"As high-profile merger plans proliferate in the wake of the credit crisis, one problem seems to be overlooked: corporate mergers fail more often than marriages."**[48]

The other people who become significantly wealthier from M&A activity are company executives. Those in the acquired company can often leave with healthy pay-offs if they back, rather than oppose, the deal. Sometimes they can make more money if they fight against it, usually by vociferously claiming the bid undervalues their company. This either forces the bidder to up their bid giving executives more for their shares or else they'll be offered even larger dollops of shareholders' money to drop their opposition and leave for pastures new. Many executives in acquired companies just play-act pretending to be against the deal in order to push up the amount they'll get paid to go quietly. As for executives in the acquiring company, they suddenly have bigger empires to run, more money to spend, greater social status and increased responsibilities. Naturally they and their acquiescent remuneration committees feel that increased responsibilities necessitate much larger salaries and more healthy bonuses. Bosses will give all kinds of excellent-sounding reasons for selling to, buying or merging with another company – economies of scale, cross-selling opportunities, cost-reduction potential, improving management capability, diversification, increased market share, synergies, access to new technologies, acquiring new products and so on and so forth. But all too often, the real motivation is rapid enrichment and self-aggrandizement of the main players involved – bankers, executhieves and accountants – and in over two thirds of cases the deal is not beneficial to the interests of us ordinary savers.

The emerging markets question

Every decade or two, unit trust fund managers and obedient personal finance journalists work themselves up into a bit of an excited lather over how easy it is for us to make money by investing in emerging markets. We're told that these countries are growing much faster than the major economies, that they all have a rapidly increasing middle class and that their stock markets are set for explosive growth. Sure enough, lots of investor money pours into emerging markets funds, pushing up prices and thus proving that the cheerleaders were right. Then follow more articles extolling the profits made in emerging markets and more unit trust ads showing how fast other people's money is increasing. Seeing the amounts of money being made by the first-movers, many more savers jump on the bandwagon and prices go up even further. So everyone seems to be doing well. But the key question is whether emerging markets price rises are supported by growing companies making profits and distributing some of this to shareholders or whether they are just bubbles which are inflated by vested interests and a bloodrush of savers' money, but which will burst as soon as demand drops.

In the short term, you can make money by finding someone else who will pay more for a share than you did. But in the longer-term, savers can only really grow their wealth from companies making profits and then paying decent dividends to their shareholders. Yet companies in emerging markets often have little incentive to worry about shareholders' wealth. For a start, many emerging markets don't quite have the same levels of corporate governance as more advanced countries – basically their economies and stock markets are rotten with corruption, enriching insiders at the expense of ordinary savers. Moreover, in a lot of countries just a few families run much of the economy and they are hardly eager to give money to shareholders which they'd rather keep for themselves. In Korea, for example one founding family runs a *chaebol* which controls almost a third of the Korean stock exchange. Shareholder dividends in Korea are shockingly low at just 1.35 per cent. There are similar situations in many other emerging markets.

> "The most obvious evidence of the *chaebols'* contemptuous attitude towards shareholders is their record on paying dividends. Korean stocks might look good value on other measures but their yields are pitiful."[49]

Unless you can find a good reason why a company's managers should give you as a shareholder a chunk of their profits, instead of putting the money in their own bank accounts, then however attractive that company's business prospects, there's no point buying its shares.

Reason 33

We trust accountants to check the accounts

Few of us will ever have the time, energy or knowledge to read through and understand the annual accounts produced by the companies in which our money is invested. After all, some can be three or four hundred pages long. Moreover, it's difficult to get behind the photos of happy executives, the glowing descriptions of their management genius and brilliant business strategies, the mass of almost impenetrable figures and the pages of obscure accounting notes to find out what is really happening. But we do expect the unit trust and pension fund managers who handle our money to use company accounts to identify where our savings should be invested and which companies are basket cases to be avoided. Yet a string of extremely dodgy events at huge companies including Enron, Global Crossing, the Bank of Credit and Commerce International, Parmalat, Equitable Life, Barings, WorldCom and many others suggest that having accountants give a company's accounts their stamp of approval may not be quite as reliable an indicator of financial strength as we might have hoped. Our justifiable worries about the value of accountants' work were probably reinforced after the 2007 banking crisis when many banks like Lehmans, HBOS and the Royal Bank of Scotland were given glowing approvals by their accountants and then promptly imploded.

"All distressed banks received a clean bill of health from their auditors and within days some were

asking the government to bail them out."[50]

In the mess that followed, we ordinary savers lost many tens of billions as the value of our savings and pension funds collapsed, interest rates dropped through the floor and the government bilked us to reward the banks for their failure. We may feel a lot poorer following the economic maelstrom, but for those fortunate enough to work in the financial services industry, the bonuses just kept on flowing. As we nurse our financial wounds, we might be forgiven for wondering how the world's economic system came so close to collapse when all the major players in the disaster had all been apparently checked by their auditors and found to be in rude health when many were actually at death's door or beyond. We might also be tempted to ask how the accountants, who failed to spot the fact that many banks were bankrupt, managed to escape without a scar during the years of financial carnage following the 2007 collapse. In fact, not only did they emerge unscathed, they actually made billions sorting out the failed banks that they had previously declared to be fighting fit. As one leading accountant remarked, 'auditing has had a good crisis'.[51]

Big Four, big bucks

The worldwide accounting industry is dominated by just four firms, commonly known as the Big Four – PricewaterhouseCoopers (PwC), Ernst and Young (E&Y), Deloittes and KPMG. There used to be the Big Five, but Andersens was blown away following its over-enthusiastic involvement in the Enron scam. These four accountancies audit over ninety per cent of the world's top companies and have combined earnings of over £35 billion a year making them economically more powerful than more than two thirds of the countries listed by the World Bank. Their enormous size and financial muscle allows these four leviathans to dictate terms to regulators and governments ensuring they can generate unbelievably large sums of money for their partners while avoiding any liability for things like negligence, incompetence, greed, tax avoidance or deliberate fraud.

Two steps to accountancy heaven

In theory, the role of auditors is very clear – by law, companies were required to have their accounts checked each year so that outsiders like tax authorities, customers, suppliers, shareholders, unit trusts and pension funds could have confidence that the accounts give a 'true and fair view' of companies' activities. So it would be reasonable to expect that auditors were in a way working for us outsiders ensuring that there was no monkey business going on in the companies they were supposed to check. That probably used to be the case fifty years ago. However in the last half century, the big accountancies have managed to push through two major changes to their legal responsibilities that have made their role as auditors immensely profitable for them but largely worthless for anyone naïve enough to believe they could trust the results of company audits.

Step 1 – Avoiding liability

When the 1948 Companies Act gave accountancies belonging to a few trade bodies a monopoly for carrying out audits, accountancies were not allowed to trade as ordinary limited companies. The fear at the time was that giving accountancies limited company status would reduce their incentive to do proper audits as they would face little risk of any major financial loss if things turned nasty. Instead, it was felt that by making accountancies operate as partnerships with the partners having unlimited liability for any negligence or dishonesty, this would give the partners strong incentives to police each other's work as failure by one partner could have serious financial consequences for the others.

For years the big accountancies lobbied to have their unlimited liability status changed. But in spite of huge sums given to helpful politicians who for legal reasons we cannot name here, these efforts got nowhere. Then in the mid 1990s the accountancies had a brainwave. By offering all kinds of inducements, they effectively bribed or hijacked the Jersey government to allow them to register themselves as Limited Liability Partnerships (LLPs) in Jersey. This allowed accountancies to keep all the wonderful tax advantages of operating as partnerships while giving the partners the kind of protection against financial loss that directors of limited companies had.

The law that was passed was written by the lawyers for one of the accountancies, not by anyone actually in Jersey. Two Jersey politicians bravely fought against this obvious abuse of their legislative process but were ostracised by those hungry for the financial benefits that some cash-rich, extremely friendly accountancies could offer the island. Once the accountancies had achieved LLP status in Jersey, they were in a position to give the British government an ultimatum – either the government allowed them to operate in Britain as LLPs or the accountancies would consider relocating their businesses to Jersey thus depriving the British state of considerable tax revenues. The British government caved in almost immediately and the frightening prospect, for accountancy partners, of unlimited liability was gone for ever. As for Jersey's hopes of getting the accountancies to relocate to the island, well once the British government had given in to the accountancies, they had little use for Jersey's help any more.

Step 2 – Avoiding responsibility

Originally the purpose of published company accounts was 'to enable investors and creditors to make predictions of future cash flows, earnings and performance'.[52] Auditors were meant to check that company accounts were reliable. However, the accountancies used a legal case in 1990 to get the British Law Lords to redefine their responsibilities. In their less than infinite wisdom, the Law Lords weasel-worded their judgement when they decided that the audit report was only done to enable shareholders 'to exercise their rights as members of the company (e.g. vote at annual general meetings) and not to enable them to make investment decisions'.[53] This meant that auditors only had a duty of care to the company they were meant to be auditing and had no responsibilities at all to investors, stock markets, tax authorities, regulators, suppliers or anyone else who might have thought they could rely on companies' accounts being in any way accurate or reliable.

Changing the role of auditors from being honest cops charged with exposing any wrongdoing by companies into servants of the companies they were meant to be checking was equivalent to making the police responsible only to the criminal gangs they were meant to be policing. Of course, this was complete madness. But it was wonderful for the accountancies as it almost completely removed any chance of anyone being able to sue them for any negligence or dishonesty. So now most auditors' reports will include the sentence: 'To the fullest extent permitted by law, we do not accept or assume responsibility to anyone other than the company and the company's members as a body, for our audit work, for this report, or for the opinions we have formed.'[54]

If ever there was a get-out-of-jail-free and make-lots-of-money-in-the-process card for accountancies, this was most definitely it.

Your humble servant

By hugely limiting both their liabilities and their responsibilities, accountancies have created a unique working environment for themselves. Most other professionals – lawyers, engineers, architects, doctors – can theoretically be held responsible for negligence or dishonesty and so need some kind of professional indemnity insurance. Although most accountancies will also have insurance, this is largely unnecessary as whatever they get up to, accountancies are pretty much untouchable. This has led to a situation where accountancies seem somewhat reluctant to say unpleasant things about their clients, the companies they are meant to be policing, as to do so might lose them their multimillion-pound fees. Moreover, most of the Big Four sell all sorts of other services to their clients – consulting, computer systems, environmental audits, tax advice and so on. For example, from 2000 till HBOS's ignominious collapse, the bank was reported to have paid KPMG £55.8 million for audits and £45.1 million for other stuff. Over the same period, Lloyds TSB apparently handed over £97.4 million to PwC for audits and £50.5 million for other work. Meanwhile at RBS, Britain's biggest bankruptcy, Sir Fred Goodwin's former employer Deloittes were reported to have earned £31.4 million for the 2007 audit, rising to £58.8 million for the 2008 audit plus an additional £21.1 million for other services. Many of these add-ons are much more profitable than the boring job of ensuring the beans have been counted correctly. Furthermore, most larger accountancies operate what's called an 'eat what you kill' bonus policy – the size of partners' and managers' bonuses depend on how much work they personally can sell. All this might lead ordinary people to wonder whether the accountancies are really checking their clients' accounts with the rigour of a Sherlock Holmes on speed or whether they are actually willingly and lucratively complicit in giving a nod and a wink to every accounting wheeze their clients dream up so they can pocket huge fees and bonuses from being as helpful as possible to clients whose behaviour they should be policing.

Faced with the collapse of several of Britain's heavily audited banks, our useless politicians did start to scratch their heads, wonder what had gone wrong and even question the value of audits done by the accountancies. The Treasury Select Committee noted: 'The fact that the audit process failed to highlight developing problems in the banking sector does cause us to question how useful audit currently is.'[55] However, the accountancies have huge political clout and they give generously to the main political parties. So perhaps unsurprisingly, despite the greatest banking collapse in British history, no action has been taken to make accountancies in any way either responsible for their highly-paid work or liable for any losses incurred by people who have relied on auditors' professional opinions of companies' accounts. There is anecdotal evidence that many of the smaller accountancies, who are not desperate to sell other services to their clients, often do quite a reasonable job with their audits. But the Big Four seem to have become vast, poorly-regulated, tax-avoiding, responsibility-ducking, politically powerful, oligopolistic money-making monsters whose work cannot be relied on any longer.

Reason 34

We attend a free investment seminar

Investment seminars are much more common in the US than Britain. Research done there showed that about eighty per cent of Americans over sixty had received invitations to investment seminars with sixty per cent having received six or more in a three-year period. Around a quarter of those approached attended one or more seminars with about one in ten attendees actually going ahead and buying whatever was being sold. But now the number of companies offering free investment seminars in the UK seems to be on the rise and there have already been several cases where people have been duped out of large sums of money, sometimes several hundred thousand pounds

Investment seminars often masquerade as being educational, claiming they will teach attendees how to grow their money or how to avoid investing mistakes or how to plan for a comfortable retirement. But they are really all about aggressive selling and most will use similar tricks to hustle attendees into parting with their money. The majority claim to be revealing secrets that most people don't know, promise high returns with little to no risk and use high-pressure sales techniques to extract money from attendees. One of the most exciting I found promised to reveal 'the forbidden investment secrets that could give 17,000 per cent' returns. Most will try to frighten people into immediate action at the seminar by suggesting that there is a rapidly closing window of opportunity - typically presenters will use well-worn manipulative phrases like: 'there are only a few places/properties left', 'I can offer a discount to the first five people who sign up', 'today is your chance to get in on the ground floor' and 'if you don't act quickly, too many people will get in on the act and the price will shoot up'. The last thing these salespeople or hucksters want is for their audience to take the time to think about what is being pushed and discuss it with friends, family or advisers. They want our money, they want a lot of it and they want it fast, there and then.

There seem to be three main types of investment seminars – those trying to sell investments and investment management services, those hoping to lure people onto expensive courses and/or buy books and CDs and those which are outright scams designed to steal attendees' money.

The investment opportunity of a lifetime!

The most common seminars are aimed at enticing attendees into putting their savings into insurance products or annuities which pay the seller high commissions of anywhere from five to ten per cent. Or else they are flogging more questionable investment schemes like properties, land or exotic foreign bonds where the sellers' cut can be much higher. One expert in the US who made a living selling financial planning services wrote that he usually set a target of drawing in about $1 million in investors' money from each seminar, earning him $50,000 to $100,000 in fees per seminar. In an article giving advice to other financial sellers he revealed a few of his tricks for drumming up interest and convincing attendees to buy. Amongst other things he proposed that they should use punchy titles for their seminars like *6 financial mistakes to avoid in retirement* or *How to avoid running out of money*; should discredit attendees' current financial advisers; and should 'show them you are an impartial adviser and want them to do the best thing for their situation'.

"Even if you show people the greatest ideas in the world at your financial planning seminar, they will

take your ideas back to their current adviser. So in the nicest way, you must discredit their current adviser and show why you are better. Here's how you do it..."[56]

In addition to the usual promises of high returns with little risk, many investing seminars will tout offshore schemes claiming that these will allow investors to avoid taxes. But offshore products tend to be complex, expensive and seldom give sufficient tax benefits to justify their high costs. Moreover, presenters tend to solicit fairly large upfront amounts - they are often not interested in people who can only afford small monthly payments.

Studies done by US regulators found that most seminars made 'misleading or exaggerated claims'. As one investigator remarked, 'every rock that we turned over seemed to have a bug or worm crawling out underneath.'

Learn to make money

Each year many thousands of people in Britain attend seminars that will supposedly teach them how to make money, usually by trading in shares, property or foreign exchange. The companies are quite clever with their advertising. They don't promise to make their customers rich. Instead they will claim something like, 'This is not a get-rich-quick scheme. It is designed for people who want to leave full time employment and trade for a living and who are serious about sustainable wealth creation.'

These sessions normally last for about two hours and are actually aimed at persuading attendees to sign up on one- to two-day courses often costing several thousand pounds. Though with some companies that's just the start of a longer process of taking money from their customers – many of those who do go on the courses find that they learn very little as these courses are just further hard-sell sessions designed to make them pay an additional £10,000 or more for further supposedly 'advanced training' plus various computer systems, CDs and books that should allow them to invest or trade successfully.

The four seminars I attended all followed pretty much the same pattern and consisted of the presenter taking the audience through four main parts – telling a bit about their own personal story, revealing a few trading secrets, kicking people into action and trying to close the sale by getting a few attendees to sign up immediately while they're still hot to trot at the thought of all the money they're about to make.

When talking about why they were running the seminar, each of presenters claimed to have been in a successful career in a large company, but to have felt unhappy at being a salary slave making money for some big organisation rather than for themselves. They then told us how they had been liberated when they found out about whatever course they're selling - shares, foreign exchange or property. All four said that they didn't work for the company offering the training, but had been 'invited' to come along and tell us about how they went on the course and learnt to make so much money that they could give up their day jobs and spend most of their time either becoming wealthier or else travelling round the world and pursuing their hobbies. Later, when I checked the presenters' Facebook pages, I found that their real life stories were not quite the same as those used in their presentations.

Next came about thirty minutes giving us glimpses into the wonderful secrets of the infallible investing or trading systems we would learn if we went on the courses offered by the companies the presenters said they didn't work for. These were actually quite interesting and informative showing how to build up a property portfolio or else spot trading opportunities, place trades and limit potential losses using stops. However, I found out afterwards that all the information was available for free from the Internet and from firms operating shares and foreign exchange trading sites.

"But almost all the information taught at education courses costing thousands of pounds could be found for free, or at little cost, in the Internet or in books."[57]

One of the key messages in this section of the presentations was that nine out of ten people lost money because they just followed the herd. But that once we went on the courses they were selling and we discovered the secrets of successful investing or trading, we could make money at the expense of the suckers who would keep on losing.

A large part of all four seminars was given over to the 'do it now' section. In this, the presenter turned from financial expert into a motivational speaker and spent the time trying to goad us into action, asking things like, 'how much do you want this?' and 'why haven't you done this?' and 'every day hesitating is a day missed' and 'you must make the change' and 'this is only for people who can make decisions, if you can't make decisions, you can leave whenever you want, that's ok'. In three of the four seminars we were played a short video ostensibly showing people just like us who had taken the courses and were now making lots of money. One of these supposedly successful students was clever enough not to mention what exactly he was trading, so his videoed testimonial was used twice by one company – both in a seminar on shares trading and in another selling a foreign exchange trading course.

Each seminar ended with a fairly pushy attempt to get us to sign up on the spot rather than going away and thinking about it. One offered a package of training, books, CDs and coaching worth £2,995 plus VAT for just £1,997 plus VAT. Another came with an even more amazing deal – a whole training package worth £6,235 plus VAT, coincidentally also for just £1,997 plus VAT. We were told the dates of the next few courses and informed that there were only two or three places left on each course. I reckon that three or four people in each session did sign up on the spot in order to take advantage of these apparently spectacular deals. What I found most worrying was that those who did register for the courses looked like the people in the audience who could least afford it. As one US regulator commented, 'They are preying on the weakest people financially. You see a disproportionate number of minorities and immigrants.'[58]

Take the money and run

Some seminars are apparently deliberate scams where the presenters convince attendees to invest in completely fraudulent schemes. Work done in the US suggested that just over one in ten investment seminars were out and out theft. It seems incredible that someone would attend such a seminar and then willingly hand over five- and six-figures sums to a complete stranger to be invested in off-plan, new-build properties in the UK and Spain or in promissory notes for Turkish investments or in building a new holiday resort in Brazil. But people apparently do and when they do, they lose an awful lot of money. One group of scammers in the US managed to grab $20 million before they were rumbled and in Britain a property investment firm took at least £11 million off people who thought they were investing rather than just being robbed. When investors started complaining about their losses, the owners claimed they had done nothing wrong and said they would defend themselves aggressively against any legal actions brought by those whose savings had skilfully performed an impressive disappearing trick.

Reason 35

Too many of us fall for investment scams

A key aim of *Pillaged* has been to focus on many supposedly respectable mainstream ways we invest our savings – bank accounts, ISAs, unit trusts, life insurance, pensions, with-profits schemes, stock market bonds, funds of funds and so on – to expose how these make massive profits for financial industry insiders, but seldom give us the frequently advertised and sometimes promised levels of returns. We may not make as much money as we thought we would with these products, but at least we shouldn't lose all our savings. However, the book would not be complete if I didn't briefly touch on just some of the many scams aimed at us savers – schemes designed to steal most if not all of the money they can from us.

Theft is big business

Probably everyone with a home or email address will have been approached by scammers of some description. What might be surprising is the number of people who seem to fall for scammers' tricks. It's difficult to get accurate figures of the scale of financial fraud because it's thought that less than one in five people who've been conned ever report the crime to the police or other official bodies. Many are so embarrassed to have been taken in and to have lost money that they don't even tell their family or friends. The best estimates I could find suggest that about four million people in Britain respond to money-making scams each year with around half losing £50 or more. Of these, up to 100,000 have lost more than £5,000 each. Police believe that in total at least £1 billion a year is stolen from us by scammers – around £4 million each working day. Though, as scammers don't seem to take weekends off or holidays, perhaps this should just be £2.7 million a day. If you're one of those who have lost out to financial fraudsters, perhaps you shouldn't feel too bad - in the US in 2009 a university professor who was the author of a respected book about gullibility admitted in an article written for the *Wall Street Journal* that he had invested about a third of his retirement funds with the now-imprisoned Bernard Madoff.

Small but perfectly formed

The majority of scams are fairly small, netting only a few hundred pounds from each victim. The most common are the Nigerian 419 scams, named after the penal code number relating to this scam in Nigeria, where for a time many of these originated. Typically you receive an email from someone like Mrs. Aminata Abdullahi, or a person claiming to be her, who is apparently 'wife to the deceased former Head of Delegation to the World Bank in West Africa'. This person contacted me because he or she wants me to help him or her recover $8 million paid in bribes to her husband as she apparently has a bit of a problem – 'the code of conduct bureau forbids him or his wife to acquire such amount of money.' Not only will I get thirty per cent of the money for myself, but she'd also like my help investing the rest for her and her only son. It all seems pretty good given that she assures me (and probably hundreds of thousands of others) 'I will not fail to bring to your notice that this business is risk free and doesn't have any negative implication.'

Should I reply to Mrs. Aminata Abdullahi, I imagine I will have to send her some money for all kinds of costs before I can get sight of the $8 million. Were I to be taken in, I doubt I would ever see any of my money again and certainly none of the promised $8 million. Plus, Mrs. Aminata Abdullahi may actually be an extremely large and threatening Nigerian or Ghanian man with some pretty unpleasant friends, perhaps not the sort of person with whom to do any kind of business. If I don't fancy working with Mrs. Aminata Abdullahi, then I could instead try Sour Aziz, Suleman Bello, Zube Kabel, Jacques Sekou, Larry Mussa, Moses Favour or any of the many others who have approached me with similar propositions in the last fourteen days. Of all these, perhaps Zube Kabel may well be the most enterprising as he/she claims in one email to be a 22-year old female medical student from the Sudan and in another he/she is apparently a Mr. and is the credit officer in a bank in Burkina Faso. Or perhaps I am being overly suspicious and actually Zube Kabel is just a common name for both men and women in the Sudan and in Burkina Faso.

In a delicious twist to this scam, some victims have been contacted through emails purporting to be from other victims. These have claimed that they were hiring detectives to get the victims' money back and they solicit the recipients for money to pay for the detectives' services. Naturally, these too are scams. So some people are being bilked twice.

Big but not beautiful

The two larger scams targeted at ordinary savers are probably boiler rooms and mailings offering investment opportunities. Although these may seem to be ridiculously and obviously blatant cons, they apparently do work and they transfer a lot of ordinary savers' money into the welcoming pockets of their perpetrators.

Boiler rooms got their name because they were originally run from small rooms in hot countries, often the Far East. Nowadays there are boiler room scams targeting British savers from any countries where they can get find English-speaking staff who are sufficiently low-life that they are prepared to spend hours a day trying to cheat us out of our money in return for commissions of anywhere between ten and twenty per cent. Some boiler rooms sell bogus shares in non-existent companies and, once they've got enough money, close down and just disappear with suckers' cash. Others specialize in real investments. But these tend to be things like Reg-S shares – little-known warrants in real US companies which are aimed at overseas investors and always trade at a much lower price than the regular shares. The advantage of offering shares in a company which actually exists is that if a saver Googles the company to check what they are being sold, the company will look legitimate and the shares being offered will seem invitingly cheap. However, should they later try selling their shares, the scammers' marks will get little or nothing back. But that may not be the end of the victim's misery. As with so many scams, once a scammer has found someone they can take for an expensive ride, they often can't resist going back for just a little bit more. So victims of boiler roomers may find themselves being contacted by the same or other scammers offering to buy their shares at very attractive prices, providing the scammees first send an administration fee. Of course, the administration fee disappears and the scammees are left with their largely or totally worthless shares and even less money than they originally had.

"I would always start off by telling cold-call targets they had responded to a marketing survey in the past year – never true, as we got names and numbers from UK shareholder lists."[59]

One might think that only a fool would fall for someone phoning up out of the blue trying to sell shares at supposedly bargain prices. But many boiler rooms get their lists of names of people to call from the shareholder registers of major companies. One list of 38,000 names and contact details was found to be used by up to 150 different boiler room operations. So the targets are not financial baboons but often reasonably savvy investors with experience of buying shares in legitimate businesses. Almost unbelievably the average loss is estimated to be about £20,000, but some people have lost over an incredible £100,000.

> **"The profile for your average victim of a share fraudster is over fifty, male, with ten plus years' worth of share buying experience."**[60]

Though boiler rooms tend to concentrate on selling shares, some offer other things like investments in properties or fine wines which may or may not exist. But even if they do exist, they are probably worth considerably less than the prices paid by the scammees.

Boiler roomers need to go to the time, cost and effort of personally contacting their victims to try to rip them off. So the number of people they can rob each week is limited to the number of suckers they can find amongst the people they can call. Companies offering investment opportunities, on the other hand, can send spam emails to hundreds of thousands of targets in a few seconds at little cost, so they are probably more common than boiler roomers. The investment opportunities hawked by these fraudsters can be many and varied. Recently I've been tempted by offers of land in Brazil with returns of 'between 174 and 257 per cent', farmland in the Ukraine that's shooting up in value due to the world's increasing demand for food, gold, silver and various high-price metals that due to my extraordinary ignorance I've never heard of, fine wines and moringa tree plantations (whatever they are). In each case, apart perhaps from the moringa trees, the promises made do sound plausible. But as with any investment tip, why would someone be spending time and effort telling complete strangers about dead cert money-making opportunities they've discovered? Yet this seems to be a question some savers forget to ask either themselves or the people trying to take their money.

Another common ploy is to tell us that we are being given secrets not available to any other investor (apart, of course, from the other few hundred thousand people getting the email) pushing shares in smaller companies which are apparently about to experience explosive growth. Often these will be in oil and gas firms that are supposedly about to announce huge new discoveries or in biotechnology companies that have made major breakthroughs they are apparently going to license to one of the larger pharmaceutical companies. The stories spun by these spammers may appear credible to the credulous. But usually the spammers will be doing a 'pump and dump' – they'll have bought some shares themselves and, as the companies are extremely small, a few suckers falling for their promises will push up the price allowing the scammers to sell out leaving the johns holding almost worthless garbage.

The other age-old scam is offering us investment tip-sheets and newsletters which will earn us two hundred, three hundred or even five hundred per cent a year. We may be told that the normal subscription price is £499 a year, but if we respond immediately we can get the newsletter for the amazing price of just £199. Sometimes the offer is even more enticing, for example, 'Add up all this research and exclusive reports and it would cost you £3,667 for a single year. For a decade of all this research you would pay £36,670. But if you join today, you pay just £5,447. That's all you'll pay – ever – except for a small annual maintenance fee of £129.' All in all, this must be a great deal as, 'By year five you'll have saved over £12,342 and by year ten £30,032!'

Just the other day, I received a leaflet inviting me to: 'harness this hidden G-Code, and you could force the stock market to pay you £35,000-£40,000 a year in your spare time, by tapping a few keys two or three times a month'. The person who had 'finally cracked the Holy Grail of investing…a hidden code that dictates EVERY stock market movement' was offering to share 'the G-Code' with me providing I wasn't a 'novice', 'dreamer' or 'halfwit'. Having not had much success with the G-Spot, I decided to give the G-Code a miss. But who knows, perhaps I have just missed the get-rich chance of a lifetime.

These tip-sheets and newsletters are sometimes run by 'pump-and-dumpers' or they may just make their money from subscriptions. Either way, the only people likely to emerge wealthy from tip-sheets are those doing the tipping and not those believing the tips.

Part 4

Our pensions may not have a happy ending

Reason 36

We hope that healthy savings will give us a healthy pension.

First *LOL* then *OMG*

If you're one of the few fortunate people that still have a final-salary pension or else if you've won the lottery of life by becoming a politician or by working for the public sector, then you've no need to read this section. You'll probably live a life of relative luxury without a financial worry in the world both before and after you retire. But if you're one of the majority of us who have to save for their own pensions, then it might be advisable to invest just a few minutes considering how comfortably or otherwise you will be spending your twilight years.

Figure 1.a showing our rising life expectancy should make most of us very happy. We're living longer healthier lives. A man turning sixty five in 1980 could expect to live till about he was seventy eight and a woman till she was eighty two. It's projected that a man reaching sixty five in 2020 should hit almost eighty six and a woman over eighty seven. Most readers of this book will probably live five to ten years longer than these national average figures as they will generally be in better health than the average poorly-educated, obese, junk-food-guzzling, binge-drinking, reality-TV obsessed, couch potato Brit. However, Figure 1.b should worry more than a few of us. This shows how much we're likely to get if we bought a pension annuity at sixty five. In 1980 a £100,000 pension pot would have netted us about £17,000 a year for the rest of our lives, but in

2011 this had fallen to around £6,000 or even less with some annuity companies. That's a drop of almost two thirds in just thirty years. As life expectancy rises even further, we should expect continued falls in annuity rates, although thankfully the decline seems to be slowing as rates can hardly go down much further.

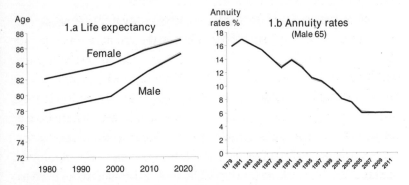

Figure 1 – Our life expectancy is increasing (LOL), but the pension we can buy with our savings is falling (OMG).

Why we'll need awfully big pots

However, the real situation many of us will face may be much worse than Figure 1.b suggests. In Figure 1.b I've taken the annuity rates for a single man buying a flat-rate income for the rest of his life. Women would get slightly lower rates as they would be expected to live for longer. However, if the person was to take a joint annuity to provide for his or her partner after their death and/or an annuity paying a pension that would rise in line with inflation, then each £100,000 would buy about half the income. For example, an inflation-protected, single-person annuity would only give about £3,300 to £3,500 a year. So, with the state pension at around £5,000 a year, if you wanted to retire with an inflation-linked income of £15,000 a year, you'd need a pension pot of almost £300,000; for £20,000 a year it would be close to £430,000; and for a pension equal to the average wage of £26,000 a year, you'd require savings of somewhere in the region of £600,000. But if you were planning to have a bit of fun in retirement and estimate this would require an income of £30,000 to £40,000, then you should be looking to save something approaching one million pounds. Anything much less than this and it's going to be a life of cheap wine, chips and caravan holidays in Clacton-on-Sea rather than champagne, caviar and world cruises.

The maths here are very simple – with annuity rates at around 3.5 per cent or less, you just need to choose the amount you want to receive each year in retirement, subtract the £5,000 that you hope you'll get from the state pension and then multiply by around thirty. So if you want £20,000 a year, you'll need £15,000 multiplied by thirty – about £450,000 in pension savings. Or, if you already have a feel for how much you'll have saved up in your pension fund by the time you stop work and you want to get an idea of your likely inflation-protected income from retirement till popping your clogs, just divide by thirty and add your state pension of £5,000.

A reality check

Now that you have a realistic idea of how much you'll need to save for a reasonable retirement – about thirty times the annual income you want – it's probably worth looking at how much most people are actually managing to save. Over the last five years, 3.2 million of the four million or so people retiring had less than £30,000 in pension savings, meaning that they'd get about £2,000 a year with a flat rate annuity and just £1,050 with an inflation-linked plan in addition to their state pension. Of the remaining 800,000 retirees, around half had savings of between £30,000 and £50,000 and only 400,000 managed to put aside over £50,000. Consumer research has shown that most people imagine they're going to get somewhere around £15,000 a year in retirement. The reality is that nine out of ten retirees can expect an inflation-linked income of around £6,000 to £7,000 a year including their state pension.

But there is also a new worrying phenomenon. Some of us are

entering retirement with debts still owing on our mortgages, credit cards, loans or bank overdrafts. Given the massive and possibly surprising reduction in earnings most of us are going to experience when we find out how small an income our retirement savings are actually going to buy, this is not a particularly smart thing to do.

We believe our pension fund's projections

One terrible mistake many of us make is to take our pension fund managers' growth projections seriously. When selling us their pension savings schemes, companies will provide glossy brochures extolling the benefits of their brilliant investing skills and enticing us with projections of how comfortably off we'll all become from giving them our money. Typically they'll do projections of the growth in our pension savings using a low rate of five per cent, a middle rate of seven per cent and a high rate of nine per cent. The only problem is that few companies have ever achieved these growth rates consistently over any longer period of time. As a whole, the industry has averaged around four per cent a year over the last fifty or so years – rather less than the five, seven and nine per cents they use to attract our custom. Over the last ten years, the industry average was just around one per cent. Even today, some companies that have only achieved one per cent or less for over twenty years are still luring in customers with the widely-used and much-abused five, seven and nine per cents.

When I was writing *Fleeced! How we've been betrayed by politicians, bureaucrats and bankers*, I rang round several pensions experts to ask what rates they thought were achievable. I couldn't find even one who thought that more than four per cent was a possibility. In 2009, my Legal & General Cash Fund got me all excited by forecasting returns of: 'Lower rate – 2.7% p.a., Mid rate - 4.7% p.a. and Higher rate - 6.7% p.a.' That sounded okay to me given that bank interest rates were so low at the time. But although I had my money in a cash fund, Legal & General actually managed to lose part

of my money once they had deducted their management charges –
none of the enticing 2.7, 4.7 or 6.7 per cent projected growth for me.

The lesson here, of course, is that we need to treat any such
projections as pure advertising fiction invented by salespeople and
marketeers and bearing no relation to what actually happens in the
real world. Unless we are prepared to accept that our pension savings
are likely to grow at somewhere around two to three or at most four
per cent a year, we risk being terribly disappointed when we
eventually decide to call on our pension savings to fund our
retirement.

Forcing us to let them steal our money

Both the last and the current governments are well aware of the
legions of people who haven't saved enough and so face pension
poverty. But with our national debt at crippling levels, the
government can't afford to look after anyone who has failed to make
sufficient provision for their old age. The Labour government tried to
introduce a compulsory pensions savings scheme. This was spun
through several versions by government spinners till it was finally
called the 'National Employment Savings Trust' shortened to the
rather attractive and comforting acronym 'NEST' with all its
reassuring associations with nest-eggs and us being looked after.
NEST would have led to workers being automatically enrolled,
forcing them and their employers to put money into pension savings.
The government needs a scheme like this to try to reduce the number
of people likely to be dependent on state handouts after they retire.
And, of course, the proposal has been enthusiastically supported by
the pensions industry as it would lead to massive amounts of money
being sliced off from around twenty million ordinary workers' pay
packets each month and handed over to them for 'safekeeping'. Even
if each of the participants in the NEST scheme only saved a meagre
£500 a year, this would give at least £10 billion a year to pension fund
sellers and managers. In five or ten years, after the NEST assets had

reached £50 billion to £100 billion, the whole system should be a fruitful source of profits for the financial services insiders controlling the money.

The NEST plan is now being reviewed by the coalition. However, with the government flat broke and with the pensions industry strongly represented in the group doing the review, we can expect the result of the review to be some kind of compulsory auto-enrolment pensions savings scheme similar to NEST. When the decision is made, we will be told by politicians, pensions experts and sycophantic reporters on ever-compliant BBC news programmes about how the new scheme will ensure we all have healthy retirement pension pots and turn our pension savings into 'a tax-free cash machine'. In fact, for most people it will be more akin to organised theft of their money as they will get nothing at all back from their enforced savings. Currently anyone on a basic state pension gets almost £30 a week (£1,500 a year) in pension credits. Plus they receive other things like council tax benefit and help with their rent. However, if they have income from pension savings, then this pension credit is reduced. Someone managing to save £45,000 could buy an inflation-linked annuity of just over £1,500 a year. But these earnings would automatically be deducted from their pension credit and other benefits leaving them not a penny better off. It is possible that pension credits might be reduced in the future if the government decides to raise the basic pension. If this happens, then making modest pensions savings won't penalise the lower paid to such a great extent. But with the way the pension credit works at the moment, it makes saving completely futile for anyone likely to have a pension pot of £45,000 or less – currently over eight out of every ten people. And when you take account of the other benefits people on the basic state pension get, for the majority of workers saving for a pension may help get the government off the hook of looking after us and may make billions for the pensions industry, but it will do less than nothing for most of the people forced to save.

Financial advisers and pension companies are so worried about the possibility of being sued for mis-selling pensions to the lower paid, that many now caution their customers using phrases like, 'A small personal pension may reduce the amount of state benefits that you are entitled to in the future.' But when the government eventually decides to force those on lower incomes to put money aside for their pensions, there are unlikely to be any such warnings.

It's off to work we go

When the state pension in its current form was introduced following the 1946 National Insurance Act, most people weren't expected to live for much more than five to ten years after retirement. So a typical life might be 20-45-10 – twenty years growing up, forty five years working and ten years getting a pension. People were spending about four times longer working and paying taxes than they would have in retirement. By the 1960s this had become more like 25-40-15. We were taking longer to get an education, spending less time working and then receiving a pension for longer. Today it's more like 25-40-20. And this is unsustainable. Neither we nor the government can accumulate sufficient money during our working years to pay for both our children's education and twenty years or more of our own retirement. Most of us have realized this has to change to something closer to 25-45-20, so we work till at least seventy. This will give us more time to save money, the government more time to collect taxes from us and also, by taking retirement later, we will be closer to death and thus may get slightly better annuity rates than are currently available to 65-year olds.

However, if you're a bureaucrat at the EU, a politician, a senior civil servant, a hospital manager or a council boss, all these pension problems must seem rather laughable. Thanks to our enforced generosity, each of us ordinary taxpayers would have to save at least £50,000 a year into our pension plans to get the same massive pensions and wonderfully early retirement that you have so considerately decided we should give you.

Reason 37

Starting saving early may be a mistake

Most of us have probably seen headlines like 'Planning For Retirement: Start Young' and 'To Get Rich in Retirement, Start Saving in your Twenties'. In fact, we're constantly being told that the earlier we start saving for our pension, the more likely we are to have a financially secure retirement. 'Save as much as you can as early as you can and you'll be off to a great start' is the message that comes from financial services companies eager to get hold of our money, personal finance journalists who are sometimes worryingly close to the companies whose products they write about and financial advisers eyeing up their juicy commissions. And this is constantly reinforced by governments hoping we'll look after ourselves in retirement as their appalling levels of debt mean they can no longer afford the burden of paying us adequate pensions. That's why most Western governments offer us seemingly attractive tax breaks on the money we put into our pension schemes – they want to encourage us to get into the pension-savings habit as early as possible.

To most of us, this 'start early' message probably sounds quite plausible. After all, surely it's common sense that the longer we save, the more money we'll be able to accumulate? But as with all tempting financial services blandishments, it's worth doing a couple of simple bag-of-a-fag-packet number crunches to check whether the persuasive 'start early' advice is actually good for our financial health or just good for those who want large chunks of our money.

Let's take the case of someone who starts saving £5,000 a year into their pension at the age of thirty. The £5,000 would probably be made up of contributions from the saver and their employer of around £330 a month plus a tax rebate from the government of twenty per cent. Over the last fifty years or so, the average pension fund has given an annual return of around four percent. However, the average fund costs at least 2.5 per cent a year in fees, management charges, dealing costs and other expenses. If we use the four per cent growth and 2.5 per cent costs and just look at this person's first ten years of savings, then by the time the saver is forty they will have put in £40,000 and the government will top this up with another £10,000 – so £50,000 in all. This money will have grown a bit and the saver would have paid about £7,500 in costs, leaving pension savings of around £54,000. Because of the fairly generous costs, the saver's £50,000 will only have gone up by around £4,000 – just eight per cent in ten years giving less than one per cent a year growth – not great even with the tax break. So the saver gets a thoroughly modest increase in value – a mere £4,000 – while almost twice as much (£7,500) goes to various finance professionals.

However, spool forward another twenty seven years to when the saver decides to retire at sixty seven. By now, assuming the same four per cent growth and just two per cent costs as many pension schemes drop their charges by half a per cent after ten years, the value of the first ten years' savings will have reached just over £90,000 for the saver, but the fees paid will have shot up to almost £50,000. Thus the first ten years' savings will have given the saver an extra £40,000, but the financial services people will have pocketed a healthy £50,000 in fees and management costs. It's debatable who has received the most benefit from this saver's conscientious decision to start putting money aside early and it's not obvious that the main beneficiary has been the saver.

You can do a similar exercise on the next ten years' savings and so on. For each ten years you move closer to retirement, the picture looks a little better for the saver and a little less unbelievably magnanimous for financial services insiders.

Sometimes the situation may be even more horrific for the saver. On my NPI pension which I started in 1989, I have to pay fees of 6.75 per cent of my first two years' contributions for thirty years until I can withdraw my money. It's not difficult to see that paying 6.75 per cent for thirty years will make quite an extraordinary dent in my money, but probably make a few people at NPI exceptionally happy.

Then there is another factor to take into account. In their thirties most people will just be paying a basic rate of tax, say twenty per cent. But by their fifties they may be paying higher rates, for example forty per cent. So, any pension savings made in a person's thirties will get tax benefits of twenty percent, but have to pay out much more in management charges. On the other hand, savings made in someone's late forties or in their fifties might get tax benefits of forty per cent and yet only attract much smaller charges as a per cent of the total saved because fund managers will be milking them for a shorter time.

All this could suggest that the hefty fees taken by pension providers make early pension savings a bit of a hiding to nowhere for a lot of savers, but a fabulous profit opportunity for the pension companies. Perhaps many of us would be better off doing something else with our money till we reach at least forty five and then, if we want to save for a pension, shove more money into our pension savings from our mid forties on.

Moreover, as explained in *Reason 7 – We're mad enough to save while we owe money*, in many cases the situation is much worse than I've described here. At the same time as someone in their thirties is putting the £5,000 a year into their pension and getting a miserable real return of less than one per cent a year, he or she is probably also paying off a mortgage or home loan costing five to six per cent a year. That surely must be a perfect example of financial lunacy – to be borrowing at six per cent a year at the same time as you're saving to get a return of less than one per cent. Yet millions upon millions of people throughout developed countries are doing precisely this. This widespread form of financial insanity makes tens of billions of pounds and euros and dollars every year for financial services firms – money that comes straight out of savers' pockets.

Of course, everyone should redo this calculation to take account of their own situation as not all pension savings schemes cost the same and some people in their thirties and forties will be higher earners paying top rates of tax and so will get more from the tax-free status of pension savings. But for many of us, in spite of what pensions experts, financial advisers, journalists, various other financial services cheerleaders and politicians say, saving for a pension in our thirties and even early forties while paying off our homes may be stupidity beyond the bounds of belief. However, even if we've paid for our homes, to get £40,000 for our first ten years' pension savings while handing almost £50,000 to a possibly undeserving financial services industry is perhaps not the best use of our money. Maybe the £40,000 to £50,000 we could put into our pension savings in our thirties would be better employed buying a larger home that we and our families could enjoy for most of our lives and then, when we retire, we could downsize to a smaller home, release some money and put it into our pension pot possibly getting tax benefits at a higher rate than we would have got in our thirties or even forties.

There may be cases where 'starting early' with pension saving could be the right thing to do. But for a lot of us it will possibly be one of the dumbest investment decisions self-serving financial professionals will ever persuade us to make.

Reason 38

We've no idea of the real costs

Charge!

Most people have no real idea how much they're paying each year to their pension management company to look after their savings. The few who think they know will probably believe that they're only paying the annual management charge (AMC) – this is usually somewhere between one per cent and two per cent, though on pensions started more than ten years ago, it may be higher than three per cent and even as much as six per cent. Before writing this section, I rang round five of our largest pension providers to check whether the AMC covered all the costs their customers would pay and all assured me that it did. However, either through ignorance or deliberately, what they said probably wasn't true. There are usually other charges taken by pension companies which are not included in the AMC. These tend to be hidden away in the small print of their contracts, if they're mentioned at all. There might be a charge for setting up the pension – possibly a one-off cost of three to five per cent, though it can be as high as ten per cent, taken straight off the amount we want to invest. Then each year there can be dealing costs as the pension manager or fund managers who are looking after our money buy and sell shares, bonds and other investments – dealing charges can include brokers' costs, stamp duty at half a per cent and the difference between the buying and selling prices of what they trade. Dealing costs can easily knock up to one per cent more off our savings. Moreover, if our pension fund manager has put our money into investment funds and hedge funds run by other management firms then their management charges will also be deducted from our savings. We should also watch out for transfer-in charges for moving money into our pension and exit charges of four to five per cent if we want to transfer our savings to another pension fund manager.

When I contacted NPI to find out what pension charges I was paying, they insisted they were only taking 1.5 per cent a year. So I asked why I had seen a document showing that the financial adviser who had sold the scheme to my employer would be collecting at least sixty per cent of my early contributions. NPI said that any fees paid to the adviser would come from NPI and not from my money. But by pushing a little harder, I discovered that I would actually be paying 6.75 per cent in charges on my first two years' contributions for over thirty years and then 1.5 per cent on subsequent contributions. Multiply 6.75 per cent by thirty years and you come to an unpleasantly large number. Some other pensions companies may be more forthcoming than NPI about the real costs we are paying, but I doubt it.

How molehills become mountains

It's possible that like me when I started to look at pension charges, you're thinking that it doesn't really matter too much if we're paying one per cent a year or two per cent a year in charges. Intuitively it feels that if we're paying two per cent rather than one per cent then our final pension will just be a few per cent smaller. So that's nothing to get too worked up about. Wrong. Someone paying low fees for their pension can end up with almost twice as much money as someone paying slightly higher fees. Because of the compounding effect of charges over time, the effects of small differences in charges are hugely magnified.

To give an example: suppose someone saves for forty years into their pension. In the first ten years they and their employer contribute just £4,000 a year, which is boosted up to £5,000 due to the tax benefits of pension savings. The next ten years they contribute £5,600 a year, which becomes £7,000 with tax rebates. Then for the final twenty years their employee and employer contributions rise to £8,000 a year (£10,000 with tax rebates). Assuming a growth rate of four per cent for their funds, this person would have accumulated £630,000 with a low-cost fund charging just 0.5 per cent a year. However, if they were paying 1.5 per cent in charges, they'd only reach £508,000. So, just a one per cent difference in charges would lose them £122,000, just under a quarter of their savings. If they had a higher-cost, possibly older pension charging three per cent a year, they'd be left with £375,000. The difference between the low-cost and higher-cost schemes would reduce their savings by a massive £255,000, a loss of over forty per cent (see Figure 1).

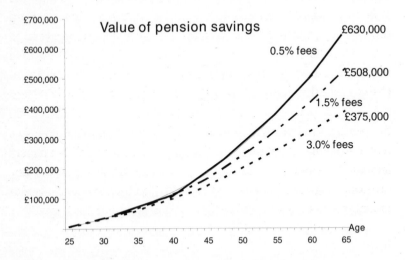

Figure 1 – Small differences in fees paid on pension funds can lead to enormous differences in the amounts left to buy a pension

The person paying just 0.5 per cent a year in charges could buy an income for life of £37,800 while the one paying three per cent would have just £22,500. If they wanted an inflation-linked pension, then the low-cost pension would give over £22,000 a year while the higher-cost one just £13,000. Most people, when they get their annual pension fund statements, probably attribute the usually disappointing growth to the fund's poor investment performance. But in reality, the failure of many funds to grow by as much as the salespeople originally led many of us to expect is often due to the corrosive effects of the fees we are paying.

> **"Huge numbers of savers nearing retirement have seen any chance of a decent pension ruined by charges."**[61]

The bottom line is that you can almost double your pension by ensuring that you put your money in a low-cost scheme. Every half per cent extra you pay in fees can result in a massive reduction in your final pension pot. However, if they can just slightly push up their charges, tiny differences in fee levels can give surprisingly large amounts of our money to financial services insiders. In the example in Figure 1, the pension with 0.5 per cent fees would pay £56,000 in charges over the forty years, the 1.5 per cent scheme – £120,000 and the three per cent fund – a gut-wrenching £196,000 in charges. So the pensions industry has huge incentives to get us to swallow fees that may seem small at first sight, but over a longer period can hugely increase the amounts industry insiders can cream off from our savings. Long-term pension savings really can turn fee molehills into mountains of cash – for the pension sellers and fund managers.

Reason 39

We buy an annuity

Lifetime security or legalised theft?

In many countries, when we save for a pension we are doing a deal with the government. We are allowed to save a certain amount into our pension funds each year without paying income tax. In return we agree not to squander this money having fun with fast cars and luxury holidays, but instead to buy an annuity once we retire to ensure we have an income for the rest of our lives. Governments like annuities because they force us to provide for our old age and we don't become a burden on other taxpayers. Annuity providers (mainly insurance companies) love annuities because they are enormously profitable. However, many ordinary people have found that annuities are extremely poor value and they have often been called 'legalised theft' because they are a financial product we are forced to buy but which may benefit the finance industry a lot more than it benefits us. As one reader of a financial website commented, 'Without exception annuities are a huge rip-off. Just another extension of the pensions industry's lousy value syndrome.'[62]

It's difficult to know exactly how profitable annuities are. Most industry experts claim companies make about four per cent to five per cent a year providing annuities to us. But there are tantalising glimpses in insurance company annual reports which suggest some firms are earning around ten per cent for taking all our pension savings and giving just a tiny proportion back to us every year till we die. Moreover, regulators have repeatedly accused annuities providers of making 'excessive profits' at our expense. With about 450,000 people in Britain buying over £10 billion a year in annuities and with companies holding hundreds of billions in annuity savings, annuities provide an excellent opportunity for finance industry insiders to enrich themselves at our expense.

The British government has already loosened the rules pushing back the age we have to buy an annuity from seventy five to seventy seven. Moreover, there is talk of allowing further flexibility around the compulsion to use our pension savings to purchase an annuity. But it seems likely that there will still be a requirement for people to ensure a minimum income from their pensions savings. Currently this looks like being around £20,000 a year including £5,000 from the state pension. Given that nine out of ten of us have pension savings of £50,000 or less which would only give an annual income of somewhere between £1,600 and £3,200 above the state pension, it looks as if very few savers will actually be able to benefit from the new rules. So whatever changes are made, almost all of us will probably still have to put some of our money into an annuity.

In spite of the bad press annuities have often had, there are many advantages of an annuity over other forms of investments for people in retirement. They guarantee an income for life irrespective of stock-market performance or changes in interest rates; they remove almost all the risk of us losing our money; and they allow us to take a flat income or else link our earnings to inflation. But critics of annuities have attacked their inflexibility and cost. Once bought, most annuities cannot be changed if an annuitant's circumstances change – for example their health deteriorates, they get married or divorced or annuity rates increase. Moreover once the annuitant dies, any remaining money is kept by the annuity company rather than going to the deceased's heirs.

Mis-selling rears its ugly head – yet again

For the majority of people the basic maths will always mean

annuities will provide poorer value than if they could have put their money in a higher-interest bank account. Annuities are a way that those who die before their average life expectancy subsidise those who live longer, with the insurance company and annuity sellers taking a healthy cut of our money for themselves. So about sixty per cent of us will lose by buying an annuity while perhaps forty per cent will gain. This would probably be acceptable to most of us as annuities work just like any other form of insurance – some people will claim much more than others with everyone paying for the peace of mind from knowing they will have a guaranteed income till their death. But critics of annuities have claimed that the annuity companies seem to be profiteering from the legal compulsion that we buy their product. At the time of writing, many 'no-win no-fee' lawyers are flocking hungrily towards annuities in the hope of a very profitable legal feeding frenzy from what may turn out to be a massive annuities mis-selling scandal to rival the great pensions mis-selling problems of the 1980s where around £15 billion was paid out in compensation (see *Reason 1 – The financial jungle is a dangerous place*).

Up till 1988 most people bought annuities from the company with which they had their pension savings. Given that there was little competition for their customers, insurance firms were under no real pressure to attract people's money. So the rates they offered were dismal for annuitants but great for the companies. Following the 1988 Income and Corporation Taxes Act, companies were obliged to inform savers about the Open Market Option (OMO) which allowed savers to buy their annuities from any company and thus get the best available rates.

Perhaps surprisingly this has not been a huge success for us customers. Several studies have suggested that almost two thirds of people don't shop around and still buy their annuities from the company where they have their pension savings even though it is unlikely to offer the best annuity rates. Tables produced by the over-funded but underperforming Financial Services Authority suggest that retirees can get between ten and twenty per cent higher pensions just from choosing a provider with the best rates. For example at the time of writing, a sixty-five year-old man buying a joint annuity to provide for himself till his death and then for his wife could get a annuity as high as £6,168 or as low as £5,256 from savings of £100,000. Over twenty to thirty years, this could easily mean a difference of more than £20,000 for every £100,000 of savings between the best and worst buys.

Another worry is that too few annuitants are taking advantage of what are called 'impaired' or 'enhanced' annuities. These enable people who have smoked or are in poor health to get much higher rates, sometimes as much as thirty per cent more, because they are likely to die earlier than non-smokers. Although about twelve per cent of British retirees have smoked, only six per cent of annuitants get the higher enhanced rates. Then when you consider how many retirees have conditions like diabetes, cancer, high blood pressure, cholesterol problems, obesity and heart disease, it's clear that the majority of those eligible for enhanced annuities, perhaps a third of all retirees, don't get them and will die long before they get reasonable value from their pension savings.

This failure of customers to get the best rates is probably making the insurance companies anywhere between £500 million and £1 billion a year or more in extra but undeserved profits. This is money which the hordes of 'no-win no-fee' lawyers would dearly like to get their hands on. So they will soon be signing up retirees in their thousands to launch compensation claims against annuity providers. Should they be successful, we can expect the lawyers to become very rich indeed. But it's doubtful whether much of the compensation cash will ever trickle back down to their clients, even if they do survive long enough to see their cases resolved in their favour.

There are plenty of websites offering comparisons of annuity rates and 'Best Buy' selections. So it's not clear why so many people lose out by not buying the best annuities. Partly it's due to customer ignorance. Annuities are so complex and there are so many different types – fixed or escalating or inflation-indexed, flat-rate or with-profits, single or joint, immediate or deferred, drawdown, enhanced, guaranteed for five or ten years and so on - that many people just choose what seems to be the most straightforward option, often from the company where they have their pension savings.

Financial advisers may also have some responsibility for us losing so much money each year as they may be pushing clients towards the poorer-paying annuities in order to get their commissions for the least amount of work. With the average customer only having around £30,000, it's not worth financial advisers' time to research the best options and help a saver through moving their money to a different annuity provider for a fee that could be as low as just £300. So they advise their customers to stick with the company that holds their pension savings. Moreover, advisers may be encouraging us to buy inappropriate annuities to increase their commissions – a simple annuity may net them just one per cent of the money invested, while a more complex with-profits policy might give five times as much. Financial advisers may also advise customers to buy an annuity as soon as they retire so advisers can bank their commissions immediately. However, it's often in customers' interests to start drawing out some of their pension savings to live on while delaying buying their annuity for a few years as the older they are, the higher their eventual annuity rate will be. Moreover, many health conditions may not reveal themselves until a person reaches sixty five to seventy. So the longer someone delays buying, the more likely they are to be eligible for a higher-rate enhanced annuity.

> **"A toxic mixture of apathy and annuity mis-selling is costing pensioners thousands of pounds every year."**[63]

But most of the blame for annuitants losing well over £500 million a year probably lies with the insurance companies. Firms have been found to have given customers saving with them 'weak' and 'misleading' advice, sometimes only mentioning the freedom for the customer to buy their annuities from other companies in the small print of their usually lengthy contracts rather than highlighting it. One report found, 'While all companies must send details of the OMO to customers, the information is buried in long and complex documents, which suggest implicitly that the consumer will buy direct from their current provider.'[64] And when customers have found better deals, insurance companies have repeatedly put up obstacles preventing their customers buying on the open market. For example, they have delayed releasing savers' money for over three months so that any more competitive offer from another company lapses before the customer can complete the transaction.

Many of us may not find the seemingly arcane details of different annuity policies exceptionally exciting reading material. But a few hours spent Googling and doing some basic checks could save us tens of thousands of pounds. Those may be the best-paid few hours of work some of us will ever do.

Reason 40

We switch, they get rich

Oh no, not another scandal

The pensions industry seems to have had more mis-selling scandals than most other types of savings and investments. This is probably because of the huge amount of money we have saved in our pension schemes and the complexity of many pension products. Moreover, the vulnerability of many pensioners makes them ideal candidates for profiteering by industry insiders. At the time of writing, yet another pensions mis-selling scandal seems to be happily bubbling away. So far a few financial advisers have paid five-figure fines and it looks like about £150 million will be paid in compensation. But it's probable that this represents only a small part of the money ordinary savers have lost due to deliberately misleading advice they have been given.

This new scandal centres around insurance companies' salespeople, banks and financial advisers encouraging us to switch our pension savings either between different investment funds or from one provider to another. Those advising us to switch often have good arguments to convince us that they are acting in our interests. For example, as we approach retirement we are usually advised to transfer our savings from riskier stock-market investments to bonds or cash funds to avoid the danger of a drop in value just before we retire. Or we may have an older pension scheme with much higher charges than more modern products and so switching could save us money. Or else our current pension scheme may be underperforming and a switch could enable us to move to a scheme with supposedly better investment returns. Moreover, with people moving jobs more often than in the past, many of us can have three or four pension schemes and so bringing them together can help us keep track of them and manage our savings. One personal finance journalist recently encouraged us to 'Round up all your pension pots' and helpfully gave the names of some companies which could offer 'a flexible, low-cost pension'. But we should be very careful when there seems to be a consensus within the financial services industry about what we should be doing with our money.

Lots of lovely loot for the looters

Getting us to switch our pension savings can be extremely lucrative for industry insiders. Usually we will be charged about three per cent of our savings just to move a lump sum from one firm to another. But some companies seem to siphon off an awful lot more than that. In a leaflet entitled *Pension Consolidation – The Power of One* written 'for professional advisers only' explaining the benefits of grouping their clients' pensions into just one scheme, a major pensions provider and household name offered financial advisers a Financial Adviser's Fee of up to 7.5 per cent of any transfer payments plus up to an additional three quarters of the first year's regular premiums made into the new single scheme.

"Some financial advisers are still telling customers to move their pension from one company to another just to earn commission – and some pension providers are even encouraging advisers to switch their clients' plans with the promise of a financial kickback, which comes out of the investor's pension fund."[65]

In another case, a saver approaching retirement lost five per cent of his money (£18,000) when moving about £360,000 from a stock-market fund to a cash fund with the same pensions company. Not bad money for the financial adviser and pension provider for maybe half an hour's work. A review carried out by the Financial Services Authority of hundreds of cases of pension switching found that eighty per cent of customers had paid 'extra costs that were incurred without good reason' and in a quarter of the firms studied none of the files of cases, where customers switched, contained suitable advice.

Lots less loot for the looted

There will, of course, be many cases where it can make sense for us to switch our pension savings. But all too often our switch just makes other people rich but leaves us considerably poorer. In many pension savings schemes we pay a big chunk of the costs upfront. For example, three quarters of our first year's contributions may be taken by the salesperson and management charges are often much higher in the early years – they may be 1.5 per cent for ten years then drop down to one per cent. So by moving, we pay the high costs of the early years with each provider we choose but lose the lower-cost benefits of keeping our money in one place. It's common for pension schemes to impose early surrender charges of around four per cent. The people trying to get us to switch will probably quote the much used and abused growth projection rates of five, seven and nine per cent to claim that even if we do pay a penalty for moving we'll soon make up for any exit penalties we have to pay. However, as most pension sellers know well, the average fund only grows at around four per cent a year, so sellers' assurances are probably intentionally dishonest.

A particularly effective argument to get people to switch has been that moving from a traditional pension, where the pension company manages our investments, to a Self-Invested Personal Pension (SIPP), where we choose our own investments will give us greater freedom and better results. For some of us, this will make sense. But many of us will have neither the knowledge nor the time to choose between thousands of funds, bonds and other investments. So we will probably just gravitate towards the most commonly recommended funds and end up paying through the nose for freedom of choice and other features that we will never use.

"Insurance companies have been quite aggressive in saying to advisers: 'Get everyone to transfer their money into our SIPP and you can earn more money off it.' In some cases they simply have more charges."[66]

Other problems with switching are that older schemes may have guaranteed annual bonuses or annuity rates which newer schemes have no chance of matching; with employer-sponsored schemes, employers may be paying the annual costs, whereas once we switch we'll be paying the costs ourselves; if we're close to retirement then we've not enough time for growth in our savings to make up for the costs of switching however wonderful a new pension provider might claim to be; and some older pensions may have other benefits such as life assurance or allowing us to take out fifty per cent as cash which we'd lose if we switched. Moreover, in a rerun of the inglorious 1980s mis-selling, it has been found that some savers with final-salary pensions have been tempted to switch to much more risky stock-market based schemes and SIPPs either with promises of better returns, more investing choices or else through being frightened that they'd lose most of their pension if their employer went out of business.

Reason 41

We get caught in the retirement home trap

This last section is perhaps not directly linked to the financial services industry. But as it may help prevent your parents, your acquaintances or you from losing up to £100,000 in a single day, I thought it worth including it. After all, a loss of £100,000 would make a fairly significant dent in most pensioners' assets. The issue concerns retirement homes. Retirement homes are usually self-contained flats in a development reserved for people over sixty. These can either be for people looking for independent living or can have staff providing assistance to any residents who need help with their daily chores. Most are originally sold on 125-year leases and provide services like an on-site warden, building maintenance, communal lounges, gardens and group activities. There seem to be two main aspects of retirement homes where people should exercise extreme caution – the high prices of new homes and the ever-rising service charges and other running costs.

How to lose £100,000 in one day

I came across this little problem quite by accident. My mother was considering moving into a retirement home, so I thought I'd check a few prices. After talking to the main developers, I was struck by the apparently large difference in prices between newly-built flats and flats that were just a few years old. For example, in a well-known retirement town like Bournemouth, where there are quite a number of retirement home developments, new one-bedroom retirement flats were selling for between £210,000 and £225,000. Yet one-bedroom flats that were less than ten years old, built in the same style to the same specifications by the same developer, often within a couple of miles of the new-builds, were only fetching £80,000 to £130,000. I found a similar situation with two-bedroom flats. New ones were priced from £270,000 to £320,000, yet resales were down in the £150,000 to £200,000 range.

Of course, you could argue that new-builds should cost more as they would be in much better condition than resales and have longer leases. But in some cases, the resales were actually more inviting as they were built when land was cheaper and so had larger gardens and grounds. From comparing over twenty developments, I discovered that a retirement flat bought new, straight from the developer will lose around a third of its value – up to £100,000 – as soon as it has had just one owner. The main reason new builds are so expensive may be that developers know their customers will probably not be particularly price sensitive as they may be moving from larger detached houses into their retirement flats and may well have sold their former family homes for considerably more than they'll be paying for their retirement home. Pensioners with large amounts of ready cash are usually ripe for plucking. So a jolly salesperson rabbiting on about how wonderful retired life will be with the security of an on-site warden and such exciting activities as weekly bingo, bridge evenings and excursions to the theatre can easily gloss over the fact that new retirement flats are frequently hideously expensive. On the other hand, resales may be more modestly priced as they tend to go for a price that is closer to general market rates for similar properties. Moreover, they will often be sold by owners moving out into care homes who may be under pressure to sell fairly quickly to get money to fund their care home fees of up to £30,000 a year. Or else they may be put up for sale by families of owners who have died. These families may be interested in getting a reasonably rapid sale to avoid paying service charges for the six months or more it can often take to sell a previously-occupied retirement flat.

I asked two experts why new retirement flats were so expensive – one was an estate agent and the other worked as a seller for one of the largest retirement flat development companies. The estate agent said that in her opinion new retirement flats were a complete rip-off and only a fool would pay the prices demanded by the developers. The salesperson seemed a bit embarrassed at the question and had to think for quite some time before admitting she didn't really have an explanation but that lots of her customers were very happy with their properties and she'd love to show my mother and I round one of their new developments so we could see what a wonderful life buying one of their flats would provide.

The bottom line is that any new-build retirement home can easily lose £100,000 of its value as soon as the buyer has signed the contract to take it. So, buying a resale from a previous owner or their family can save your parents, other relatives or you an awful lot of money - just something to bear in mind should anyone in your family or social circle start thinking about moving into a retirement property.

What goes up never comes down

Many people who have moved into retirement properties have found that service charges and other expenses have a tendency to defy gravity by constantly rising at a rate that is well in excess of the general rate of price inflation. Typical charges range from around £2,000 a year for a one-bedroom flat to £3,000 a year for a two-bedroom. With assisted living, charges are more like £6,000 to £8,000 a year. But apart from ever increasing bills, management companies seem to have several other ways of relieving leaseholders of their money.

One widespread practice is to make residents pay for the warden's (or housekeeper's) flat at a rate which is astronomically in excess of the real market level. For example, one group of residents found themselves paying £21,500 a year for their warden's rent when similar flats nearby were only achieving around £12,000 a year.

Another ploy is to charge residents excessive amounts for any building or maintenance work – usually adding on a fifty per cent premium which is then split between the contractor and the management company. A further goody is to take a one per cent cut of the price when a resident or their family sells their property. Supposedly this is meant to cover administration, though raking in £2,000 in admin when a resident uses an estate agent to make a private sale of a £200,000 two-bedroom retirement flat smells much more like profiteering.

Part 5

20 tips for surviving in the financial jungle

1. Take the time.

2. Make a financial plan.

3. Test your Financial Intelligence.

4. Measure your Emotional Discipline.

5. Understand yourself.

6. Choose your personal strategy.

7. Spot the loser.

8. Find out the real cost.

9. Cut out some middlemen

10. Only bank with your bank

11. Take a pragmatic approach to your pension pot

12. The smaller your annuity, the better off you may be.

13. Separate speculation from investment .

14. Profit from pound cost averaging.

15. Test-drive your approach.

16. Beware of 'new, improved'.

17. Get real.

18. Always compare to high-interest bank accounts.

19. Protect your parents.

20. Don't believe a word they say.

Tip 1 – Take the time

Most of us will spend up to twenty five years preparing for life, forty to forty five years accumulating and spending our wealth and then around another twenty years living off whatever we have left by the time we retire. Our quality of life will depend on how well we manage our money during the sixty to sixty five years of our adulthood. Yet many of us are too busy working, looking after our families and socialising with our friends to have much time left over to think about how we can get the best returns for our money. Few people spend more than an hour a week planning and managing their finances – many use a lot less. Now that we are on our own in the financial jungle, this is a worrying situation. The result is that most of us don't read or understand the terms and conditions of the financial products which are sold to us. Then too many of us are surprised when our savings and investments fail to produce anywhere near the levels claimed by those who were excessively eager to manage our money for us. Instead of giving us reasonable returns, we discover we have been paying extortionate management charges, outrageous commissions and many other expenses we might never have been told about. Yet if we try to move our money we may be trapped by punitive exit penalties.

Unfortunately we have to change our behaviour. It would be madness not to spend at least two or three hours a week planning our finances, reading the personal finance press, understanding the strengths and pitfalls of the different saving options and reviewing the performance of our savings. This does not mean we should rush around like blue-arse flies from one savings type to another when journalists sensationalise the profits or losses to be made by various investment types. In fact, the more you read the personal finance sections of newspapers, the more you realise that most articles are just exaggerated hype and advertising poorly disguised as journalism.

So Tip One must be – schedule just a few hours a week exclusively to managing your money. You may be amazed at how much you learn and the improvement in performance you get from your savings.

Tip 2 – Make a financial plan

The first thing you should do with the time you set aside for managing your finances is to make a financial plan. Depending on how much or little you earn, or have inherited thanks to other people's hard work, making a financial plan may be one of the most sobering or exhilarating parts of understanding your financial situation. For me, it was unfortunately the former, though I didn't stay sober for long.

A simple plan might consist of setting up a spreadsheet on which you lay out all the years from where you currently are till the age you expect to die. Then you could have a series of lines containing things like the income you expect to earn before tax, income after tax, housing costs, living costs and how much you want to spend on luxuries (see Figure 1).

Age	30	31	32	33	34	35	36	37
Income before tax	£33,000	£34,000	£35,000	£36,000	£37,000	£39,000	£41,000	£43,000
Income after tax	£21,600	£22,400	£23,200	£24,000	£24,800	£26,400	£28,000	£29,600
Housing costs	£7,500	£7,500	£7,500	£7,500	£7,500	£7,500	£7,500	£7,500
Living expenses	£10,000	£10,000	£10,000	£11,000	£11,000	£11,000	£12,000	£12,000
Luxuries	£4,000	£4,000	£4,000	£4,500	£4,500	£5,000	£5,000	£5,000
Savings per year	£0	£900	£1,700	£1,000	£1,800	£2,900	£3,500	£5,100
Savings cumul*3%	£0	£900	£2,627	£2,751	£2,830	£4,754	£6,487	£8,705
Savings cumul*5%	£0	£900	£2,645	£2,785	£2,850	£4,790	£6,545	£8,775
Savings needed *3%	£4,120	£8,244	£12,491	£16,866	£21,372	£26,013	£30,793	£35,717

Figure 1 – Making a financial plan is easy, but the reality of many people's situation might come as a bit of a disappointment

Once you've listed those, you can work out how much you can save each year. Then you should calculate your cumulative savings at two potential rates of growth – perhaps three per cent and five per cent.

Unless you're really rather fortunate, you'll probably find that by the time you reach sixty five or seventy, you haven't yet saved up the half million pounds or so that you'll need to secure an income of about £20,000 in retirement. If this is the case, then you should go back to your plan and start playing with the figures to see how much more you need to earn; less you need to spend; or growth you need to achieve from your savings to hit your retirement income goal. Just for fun, I've included a line showing how much a person would need to save each year to get near to half a million pounds by the time they reach seventy assuming they save £4,000 a year in their thirties, £6,000 a year in their forties, £8,000 a year in their fifties and £10,000 a year in their sixties. For many people this bottom line might make worrying reading.

Tip 3 – Test your Financial Intelligence

Do you know the difference between unit trusts, exchange traded funds (ETFs), investment trusts and open ended investment companies (OEICs – pronounced 'oiks')? Do you know which has the highest charges? Where's the best place to buy a unit trust? Are with-profits savings and pensions better than without-profits? How much are you really paying in charges each year on your pension savings? What's the 'Rule of 72' and what can you use it for? Do you generally trust professionals like lawyers, surveyors, accountants and financial advisers? If you've invested in a company that goes belly up is it better to have your money in that company's corporate bonds or shares? How much could a 67-year-old man expect to get from a £500,000 pension pot if he wanted an inflation-linked annuity with a fifty per cent payment for his 64-year-old wife after he died – £30,000 a year, £20,000 a year or £15,000 a year? If you're in a casino and you see that on one roulette table the ball has landed on a red number seven times in a row – do you bet red or black or zero on the next spin of the wheel?

There are quite a few tests available on the Internet where you can see how much you really know about money and saving.[67] Some are rather basic, others a bit more serious. Unfortunately most are US- rather than UK-oriented, so many of the questions about things like 401ks and IRAs won't be relevant to most of us. On one UK-based test I tried, even after writing this book I only scored twelve right answers out of twenty five questions. But that put me in the top twenty per cent of people who had taken the test. Moreover, those who bothered to take the test were probably in the top ten per cent of the population in terms of their financial intelligence. Most of us assume we know much more about money and savings than we actually do and that leads us to make decisions which enrich financial services insiders at our expense. However, it's usually only years after we have bought a financial product that we realise it is returning much less than we expected while costing much more than we had been led to believe. Most of us need to test our financial intelligence, understand what we really know and don't know and then go back to Tip 1. If we are to get value for our savings, we need to spend time learning to help ourselves with our money so that others don't help themselves to our money.

Tip 4 – Measure your Emotional Discipline

Financial intelligence and emotional discipline are probably the two things which will decide if we make the most of the money we earn or if we squander it by putting it into savings and investments which just make other people rich at our expense. We can measure our financial intelligence objectively by taking various tests. It's much harder to assess our emotional discipline. How do you feel if a share or unit trust leaps up or falls by thirty per cent or more? Would you be happy putting money into a unit trust if the stock market was falling? Do you prefer to invest when prices are rising? Do you have the willpower to stay in an investment that has lost forty per cent of its value since you bought it, when all your friends seem to be doing well putting their money into something else that is performing much better? Do you believe that you are smarter than the average saver?

Each of us has to make our own decision about how well we can cope with both financial gain and loss and whether we enjoy taking risks or are risk averse. A good way to test your emotional discipline is to set up a virtual portfolio with one of the online stockbrokers. This allows you to buy and sell shares without using real money to test your skills as an investor. It's also a good way to see how you react to gains and losses. If you really want to ride an emotional roller-coaster then you should open what's called a 'demo account' with a spread betting company. This gives you starting capital of anywhere from £2,500 to £10,000 and allows you to place bets on a trading platform that functions the same way as a real spread-betting system. Some will let you run your demo for a month, some for longer. Even though the money you're playing with isn't real, you can learn quite a lot about yourself when you see how you react to winning £1,000 in one week and then losing £3,000 the week after. It can be quite an eye-opening experience. Just make sure your cat or dog isn't around to be kicked when you lose a few thousand quid – why should some poor animal suffer from your financial cock-ups?

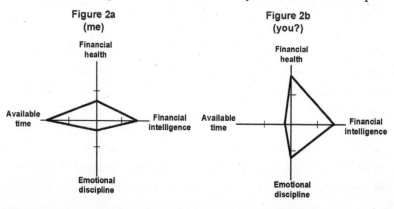

Tip 5 – Understand yourself

In order to decide how we should manage our money to survive in the financial jungle, each of us needs to understand our own personal profile as a saver. Some people might find drawing a simple kite diagram useful. On it you can rate things like your financial health – how close you are to acquiring the money you will need for your life; your financial intelligence – how much you understand about savings and investments; your emotional discipline – how much self-control you have when faced by risk, gains and losses; and your resources – how much effort you can invest each month in trying to get the best return from your money. Figure 2a shows my profile. My financial health is a disaster; I would hope I have reasonable financial intelligence after researching and writing this book; emotional discipline – virtually zero; but being unemployed I have lots of time to worry about why I'm so poor.

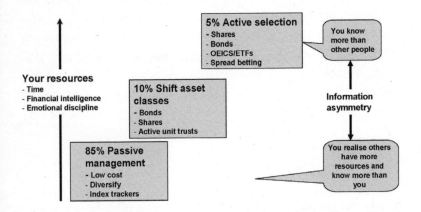

Figure 3 – Each of us must choose the savings strategy that suits our own resources

You might be more like Figure 2b, financially healthy with a good salary and lots of savings; much higher than average financial intelligence; reasonable emotional discipline; but so busy with work, family and friends that you have little space in your life to manage your money to prevent other people taking too much of it for themselves.

Tip 6 – Choose your personal strategy

Greater self-knowledge can then be the basis for each person to choose their own savings strategy – whether they would be wise to actively manage their investments to get the best returns or whether they should stick to low-cost savings schemes that just track overall markets. The more resources you have like financial knowledge, time and emotional discipline, the more you can trust yourself or others to keep moving your money to get the best returns. Though the more active your management, the more you will pay in fees and commissions. Unfortunately, most research suggests that about eighty five per cent of us should be choosing low-cost passively-managed products, about ten per cent of us should be actively moving our money between different asset classes (shares, unit trusts, bonds, bank accounts) to improve our returns and only around five per cent have the necessary resources to pick specific shares and other specialised products (see Figure 3).

Tip 7 – Spot the loser

If you're happy with getting average long-term returns for your savings – just over one per cent for bank deposits, two per cent for bonds and four to five per cent for pensions and shares, then you should be able to achieve these results without too much risk. But if you want your savings achieve higher returns, then you start playing a dangerous game.

When you buy something like a house or a holiday, hopefully you're doing a win-win transaction – the person selling the house wants to move elsewhere and you're getting the house you want or the holiday company gets your money and you're off on your dream vacation. But when you buy or sell most investments, you're usually playing a 'zero sum game' – one person will win from the transaction by buying low or selling high and the other will lose by buying too high or selling too low. If you're buying some shares you must have good reasons to believe that you are smarter than the person selling, so that you win and they lose. Similarly if a financial adviser proposes a certain unit trust or pension fund, you need to understand why the fund managers they are recommending are much more gifted than all the other fund managers against whom they'll be competing, so that what your savings gain other people's savings lose. Remember the old adage is true, if you can't spot the sucker (or loser) when you buy or sell an investment, then the loser is probably you.

In fact, trying to get above-average performance for your savings is worse than a zero sum game for savers as each time an investment is bought or sold, at least one and often several financial services insiders will be taking a cut of our money. The only certain winners in the game are those working in financial services. So for us to win at investing, we both have to spot the loser and make sufficient extra profits to cover the many costs being taken by the people managing our money. That's quite hard to do consistently over the many years most of us will try to save. Nevertheless, endless numbers of those who are eager to handle our money will claim they have the magic formula to make us winners in the worse-than-a-zero-sum investing game.

Tip 8 – Find out the real cost

It's rare for people selling investments and their sales literature to reveal the true amounts of money that they will cut from our savings. We may be told the annual management charge or the total expense ratio or some other figure. But there will usually be other expenses like dealing costs, commissions, upfront fees or exit penalties which are either just mentioned in passing or not mentioned at all. Later, sometimes several years later, when we find out we've been charged much more than we expected, we'll just be told that everything was covered in the contract. If we do then manage to get through the contract terms and conditions and understand what we've read, we'll probably find details of several charges the seller 'forgot' to bring to our attention. So, when someone is trying to lure you into a unit trust, investment bond, combination bond, pension or other financial product, it's important that you demand they list every single cost that could possibly be taken off your money. In particular, with stock-market products like unit trusts you need to know what their annual turnover ratio is (what per cent of their assets they buy and sell each year), whether this is increasing or decreasing and what this is costing you in addition to the annual management charge and the total expense ratio. Don't allow yourself to get fobbed off by someone claiming there's only an annual management charge of one or one and a half per cent. There are probably many more things you'll be paying for that the seller is less than enthusiastic about revealing in case this puts you off giving them your money.

Tip 9 – Cut out some middlemen

It seems that over the longer term a saver is likely to get about three to four per cent more a year by having their money in the stock market through shares, unit trusts or pension funds than they'll achieve from a high-interest bank account. Yet every time a financial services insider touches our money, anywhere between one and four per cent disappears into their pockets. So the only way you can actually get a better return than a high-interest bank account is to cut out as many middlemen as possible to reduce the amounts being slashed from your savings.

> **"There are some good managers out there, but a lot of the rest follow the herd and fleece their clients. An intelligent retail investor...... could outperform most of them."**[68]

If you're thinking of buying a fund of funds, why not just get sales brochures from a few funds of funds, see which unit trusts they're buying and put your money straight into those unit trusts cutting out the fund of funds managers? That should save around one per cent. Or if you want to go for some unit trusts, you could similarly request the sales bumf for those trusts, look at the main shares they are buying and buy those shares directly yourself – that could cut three to four per cent from your costs. And if you really are, like many people, in a totally dud and expensive pension scheme, you only have to fill in four or five forms to move to a scheme that is better value – doing this yourself could save you thousands.

There is one exception to the 'cut out some middlemen' advice. When buying savings schemes like unit trusts, you'll probably find you can save up to five per cent by buying from a funds supermarket or other intermediary compared to buying directly from the unit trust provider. In this case, add in the middleman.

Tip 10 – Only bank with your bank

The most expensive way to buy any savings product or insurance policy is usually through your bank. Normally banks are just selling a few products provided by other financial firms with the bank taking a generous cut of your money for itself. Depending on the product this might be around three to four per cent. In fact, even if you just want your money in a longer-term, high-interest savings account, you'll probably find your bank has some of the worst rates available. There is only one thing you should do with your bank – let them run your current account and ATM cash card. That's it. For everything else like savings, pensions, mortgages, unit trusts, foreign exchange, stock-market investments and credit cards, you should scan the market for the best provider with the lowest costs. Otherwise you're throwing your money away.

Tip 11 – Take a pragmatic approach to your pension pot

If we're to believe the government, pension companies and financial journalists then we should start saving for our pensions as early as we can and be regularly and obediently putting away as much as we can, especially as the government gives us such supposedly generous tax incentives to save. But as I hopefully show in *Reason 37 – Starting saving early may be a mistake*, making us into dutiful pension savers suits the government and makes billions for the financial services industry but may be extremely harmful for our own wealth. If your employer is paying the costs of your pension scheme or the scheme has charges of at most half a per cent, then the tax benefits of pension savings may outweigh the losses from paying a pension fund manager their costs for thirty or more years. But if you're paying 1.5 per cent or more in fees plus possibly more in other hidden costs, then any savings made in your twenties and even thirties are probably a waste of money unless you're a higher-rate taxpayer. You'd probably be much better off putting your cash into ISAs, into your house or your children's education. Then as you hit forty or more you should start thinking more seriously about pension savings.

But the really smart trick for many people wanting to save for their pension would first be to pay off their mortgage as fast as reasonably possible. Once the mortgage is gone, they could grow their savings in a cheap stock-market tracker fund or an ISA in their forties and early fifties. Then in the ten or so years before they retire they should pile their money into a low cost pension fund. For example, if someone was earning £40,000 a year between fifty seven and sixty seven, they could put this amount into their pension and get tax relief, meaning they would only have to pay £32,000 a year into their pension and the government would make this up to £40,000. After ten years, the person would have contributed £320,000 but have over £472,000 in their pension fund (assuming growth of three per cent a year after costs). When they retire, they can withdraw up to a quarter from their pension savings – in this case £118,000 of the £472,000. So contributions of £320,000 (ten years paying £32,000 a year) would leave them with £118,000 in their pocket and £354,000 in their pension – total growth of more than forty seven per cent in ten years, mostly from tax benefits. So they still get the tax advantages of pension savings without having paid high charges to a pension company for thirty years or more. There probably isn't any easier or safer way to make your money work for you rather than for those in the pensions industry.

Moreover, the costs of pension savings funds have dropped considerably over the last few years. But most of us are probably paying two, three or even four times more than we need to. We may find that we're trapped in some higher-cost schemes as they will usually have punitive penalties for any withdrawals before we reach sixty five. But some may have five or ten year anniversaries where we can move our money without paying a penalty. If you are trapped in such a scheme, you may have to leave your money where it is, but you could stop making any more contributions and instead start up a new pension savings account with one of the growing number of low-cost (around half a per cent a year) providers. With the likelihood of low stock-market returns over the next five or more years, to get any real growth in our pension savings we all need to get our charges down to below one per cent. It can be done, but we'll have to fight against all kinds of barriers thrown up by most of the more expensive pension fund management firms. If there is one area of saving where we really should be active, it's in driving down the costs of our longer-term pension savings – after all, just a one per cent cut in costs can mean the difference of £100,000 or more over thirty plus years.

Tip 12 – The smaller your annuity, the better off you may be

We will all probably have to buy an annuity at some point. In return for allowing us to put money into our pension savings tax-free, the government expects us to use that money to buy ourselves an income for the rest of our lives. Yet annuities are usually highly profitable for the companies selling them and dreadful value for us buyers. So while we should buy an annuity with some of our savings, we should probably try to limit the amount we give to annuity providers. There are a couple of ways to do this. On reaching retirement age, we are (at the time of writing) permitted to withdraw up to twenty five per cent of our pension savings without paying any tax. It's probably worth doing this and then putting this money in some other form of investment or using it to live off. Furthermore, we can delay buying an annuity till our late seventies and instead draw out an income from our pension pot each year from retirement till the date we must buy an annuity. This both reduces the money we'll give to an annuity company and increases the annuity rate we'll eventually get as we'll be older and thus closer to death. Moreover, we may fall ill before we reach our late seventies and so be able to get an enhanced annuity.

Many people approaching retirement assume they should put as much as possible into buying as large an annuity as they can afford. However, in many cases annuities are such poor value that the opposite may be true. We should save as much as we can for our pensions – after all, less than £500,000 is going to give us a fairly cash-strapped end to our time on earth – but we should probably give as little of this money as late as possible to our chosen annuity provider.

Tip 13 – Separate speculation from investment

Few people like to miss the chance of making a bit of extra money. So if we see emerging markets are booming or the price of gold is rocketing, it seems a pity not to take a punt. But the two main problems with such short-term speculation is that we often buy too high when prices are already inflated and we incur excessive trading costs by moving our money too often. One way to prevent your savings being whittled away by too many speculative moves is to split your assets into two parts, for example putting eighty per cent of your money into shares or funds that you hold for five years or more always reinvesting any dividends and then keeping twenty per cent for shorter-term speculative bets where you might move your money every two years or more frequently. Too many savers make the mistake of confusing investing (putting their money somewhere for five or more years) with speculation (jumping from one investment to another) and then find that frightening amounts have disappeared from moving their money at the wrong time and from transaction costs. If you can split your investment savings from your speculative money, you're more likely to emerge with better returns.

Tip 14 – Profit from pound cost averaging

It's almost impossible to predict when stock markets will rise or fall. After all, how many of us accurately foresaw the 2007 financial collapse and the subsequent huge rises and falls in the price of shares? One way to avoid buying when the market is too high is to do what is called 'pound cost averaging' – you put money regularly into the market over a period of years. When the market is high, you get fewer shares for your money. When it's low, you pick up more shares. If, for example, you have a share which sells for £2 for three years and then £1 for three years and you buy £1,000 of that share in each of the six years, then for £6,000 you'll have bought 4,500 shares. You'll have paid £1.33 per share, yet the average cost of the shares over those six years would have been £1.50. Because you acquired more in the cheap years, this brings down your overall average cost. With our pension savings we automatically do pound cost averaging as we tend to save similar amounts each year over a long period. But we should also think about doing this with our other savings, perhaps putting regular amounts into a cheap tracker fund, rather than taking the risk of investing lump sums when the market may be too high.

Tip 15 – Test-drive your approach

If you're going to try to get more from your savings by cutting out as many middlemen as possible, then you'll have to do more yourself. This could mean you buying specific unit trusts or even individual shares rather than paying someone else to do it for you. But before you start throwing your money around, most people should test-drive their trading approach and get some practice to improve their skills. Many companies selling share-dealing services offer free simulator accounts. These allow you to buy and sell shares and things like unit trusts without using real money so you can test your skill and see what results you would have achieved. It can be a surprisingly levelling experience to see just how many times most of us are wrong-footed by market movements.

With share or unit trust trading you're never going to either double your money or lose it all. Generally your gains and losses will not exceed ten to fifteen per cent. But if you're going to venture into the quicksands of spread betting, where you can quickly multiply your money or lose much more than you bet, you'd be more than crazy not to spend a few weeks running a 'demo account' which allows you to play around and try different trading strategies before you start generously handing over your money to one or several of the rapidly increasing number of delightfully profitable spread-betting companies.

Tip 16 – Beware of 'new, improved'

Like washing powder manufacturers, the financial services industry is forever coming up with supposedly 'new, improved' versions of its basic products in order to keep our money flowing into its hands. Bank accounts with fancy new names, stock-market investments with flashy guarantees or mouthwatering growth promises, tempting high-income bonds, with-profits schemes, easy new ways to release money from our homes – all these are vigorously promoted as if they are providing better returns for customers, when in fact they're designed, developed and sold only to improve the profits of those selling them.

A standard high-interest bank account is usually a simple and cheap transaction - the bank is lending our money out to someone else at a higher rate of interest than it gives us and takes the difference as its profit. But at least we're clear about what we're getting. When we're offered complex investment products that guarantee full return of our money, or commit to paying out a high return if some stock-market index reaches some point or other or promise high growth, there are two problems. Firstly, our returns are uncertain and secondly, the company selling these products usually has to buy some complex financial products itself to ensure it can meet its obligations to us. But the more middlemen that become involved, the more people there are taking a slice of our money. Some of the more creative financial products being pushed at us may sound 'new' and 'improved', but too often we will be sorely disappointed years after buying them when we find out just how much of our money has been spirited away. It's usually the same old washing powder, even if the box looks exciting and new and different.

Tip 17 – Get real

Since time immemorial, financial services salespeople have tried to get hold of our money by enthusing about (though usually never promising) the temptingly high returns we could make by giving them our cash. People flogging stock-market investments will typically talk about growth of seven, nine and even more per cent a year. Financial journalists will give examples of how we can grow our wealth using figures of eight or ten per cent. And most pension schemes will produce projections of how many hundreds of thousands of pounds we will have at retirement based on three rates of growth: low – five per cent, medium – seven per cent and high – nine per cent.

There are three problems here. Firstly, these rates of return have seldom actually been achieved and have almost never happened once you take account of inflation. Secondly, even if stock markets and other investments do for a time experience higher than average growth, we pay so much in charges that little of this growth ever finds its way into our pockets. Thirdly, for at least the next five years we are likely to see poor returns on any investments as individuals and governments try to reduce their debts and this constrains economic growth. Moreover, if governments decide to throw in the towel and inflate their way out of their crippling debts by printing electronic and paper money, it will be extremely difficult to make any real returns at all on our savings and investments – already most people with high-interest bank accounts are currently losing money after taking account of inflation and taxes. If things get worse, we could see years of negative or zero returns. All this suggests that you should forget about the fanciful projections of five or seven or nine per cent and instead get the seller to rework their figures using a low rate of zero per cent, medium of two per cent and high of four per cent. Then you're likely to have a more realistic idea of what you might get from your savings, investments and pension funds.

Tip 18 – Always compare to high-interest bank accounts

The mistake most people make when deciding to put money in an investment with some level of risk like a unit trust or stock-market bond is to look at the projected returns in isolation. What they should do is compare the projected returns on the risky investment to what they could receive in a longer-term (two to three years) high-interest bank account or savings bond where there is virtually no risk as savings up to £50,000 are guaranteed by the government. If you can get say two per cent from a no-risk bank account and a salesperson is talking about five or six per cent from their product, then you're actually risking your money for just a three to four per cent gain. Then when you look at the financial firm's management costs of anywhere between two to four per cent, you might find your cash is better off in a bank rather than serving as a commissions cow for the seller and a cash cow for the fund management company.

Tip 19 – Protect your parents

Many of us may feel uncomfortable talking about money matters with our parents, grandparents or elderly relatives. We probably think that mentioning money makes it look like we're testing the water to see how much we're going to get when they go to a better place. But this reticence too often has disastrous consequences for any relatives we have who are approaching or are already in the 'banana skin and grave brigade'. Because we don't know who is angling for our relatives' money and what usually specious selling arguments they are feeding them, we're unable to protect them from making appallingly-misguided and sometimes ruinous investment decisions. Financial services firms get away with flogging all sorts of garbage to the elderly – long-term stock-market bonds with high early withdrawal penalties, high-interest bonds that destroy the original capital, home equity release plans with usurious rates of interest and so on – because many older people belong to a generation that is more trusting of self-proclaimed financial experts and retirement advisers than younger people might be.

So my advice is that you should sit down with any elderly relatives, open up the subject of their money and warn them about the tricks and traps used by financial companies to loot their savings or get hold of their homes. You may feel slightly uneasy at first, but you'll be doing them a favour if you help save them from the predatory sales techniques financial firms use against some of the most vulnerable of their targets.

Tip 20 – Don't believe a word they say

The financial services industry has become a massive predatory monster. It loots unbelievable sums of money from our savings and pensions – over £413 million every single working day - making insiders fantastically wealthy and preventing the rest of us ever getting any decent returns on our money. The governments which we vote for and regulators whose elevated salaries we pay are virtually powerless to protect us from the rapacity of those who want to get their hands on our money. Occasionally there will be a scandal that is so extreme that financial firms will be forced to pay some kind of compensation. But this is usually after many years of screaming and kicking as they try to avoid their responsibilities, hold on to our money for as long as possible and benefit from the fact that some claimants will give up the struggle for their money or even die in the meantime.

Financial services insiders have carefully-prepared sales scripts to convince us to give our money to them so they can manage it for us. From exaggerated claims about high growth to deliberately concealing the real costs we will have to pay – pretty much anything goes. Of course, some of the products offered by financial services companies may be appropriate for us. But we will only get any benefits for ourselves if we can aggressively drive down the costs we pay – the real costs, not the costs we are told we will pay.

Conclusion

Tell us the truth

Give us some 'them and us' charts

While researching and writing *Pillaged* I've been concerned by the fact that the financial services industry seems to be siphoning off excessive amounts of our money – over £413 million a day – and leaving far too little for us ordinary savers. But it's often very difficult for us to see exactly how much of our money financial services insiders are pocketing. With some products we aren't told the charges. With others, what we are told – the annual management charge or total expense ratio – is usually only part of what we will actually end up paying. There is an easy solution to this problem – with every financial product we buy, we should insist that the seller does two or three projections for us showing exactly how much we will get and how much they will take at various levels of growth. For example, say we put £5,000 in a unit trust and leave it for ten years paying three per cent a year in costs – total expense ratio plus dealing costs plus half a per cent a year from the bid to offer spread. At four per cent growth, we'd gain £457 over the ten years while the fund manager would be taking £1,623. At six per cent growth, the fund manager would still be getting a little more than us – they'd take £1,807 while leaving us growth of £1,603. However, we'd be doing slightly better than the fund manager if they achieved eight per cent growth – £2,960 for us and £2,014 for them. I've produced what I've called a 'them

and us' chart to show who takes what at the three different
projected levels of growth (see Figure 1).

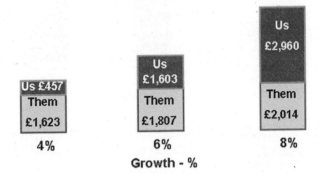

**Putting £5,000 in an actively-managed
unit trust with 3% charges**
(sharing the growth over 10 years)

Figure 1 – It should be easy for financial product sellers to do a
'them and us' chart showing exactly how much they'll get and we'll
keep from any growth in our savings

If people could clearly see a picture like Figure 1 where the fund
manager takes a big chunk of any growth, that would probably put
a lot of us off saving in a unit trust or else would make us aware of
the need to find one with lower costs. However, the 'them and us'
chart looks a lot better for us savers if we were to choose an index
tracker with charges of half a per cent (see Figure 2).

The differences between our returns on high-cost and low-cost
products look even more gruesome when we see how they affect
our pension savings. Figure 3 shows a 'them and us' chart for
someone saving £200 a month into a pension fund for thirty years
when the fund has total annual costs of two and a half per cent.
This makes it pretty clear that financial services insiders cream off
a lot of money for themselves for very little work and seem to do a
lot better than the saver from the saver's efforts to build up a
pension.

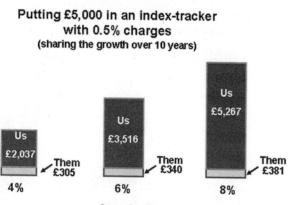

**Putting £5,000 in an index-tracker
with 0.5% charges**
(sharing the growth over 10 years)

Figure 2 – Hopefully comparing 'them and us' charts for an actively-managed unit trust (Figure 1) and an index tracker (Figure 2) shows the huge differences in charges taken from us

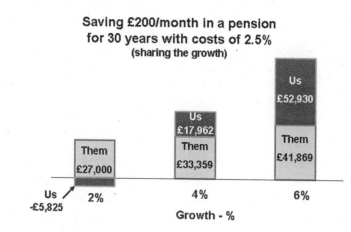

**Saving £200/month in a pension
for 30 years with costs of 2.5%**
(sharing the growth)

Figure 3 – With many pensions, half or more of the growth is being taken by salespeople and fund managers

This situation looks much better for the saver and an awful lot less overly generous to financial services insiders when we put our money into a low-cost (half a per cent a year) SIPP giving us most of the growth and costing us very little in fees (see Figure 4).

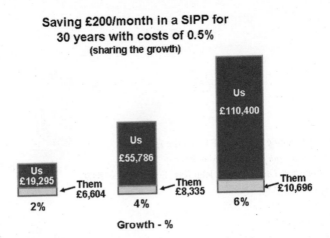

Saving £200/month in a SIPP for
30 years with costs of 0.5%
(sharing the growth)

Us
£19,295
Them
£6,604
2%

Us
£55,786
Them
£8,335
4%

Us
£110,400
Them
£10,696
6%

Growth - %

Figure 4 – With a low-cost SIPP (0.5% a year) we savers keep almost all the growth for ourselves

Financial salespeople will never show us a 'them and us chart' as we'd probably be horrified by what it showed and wouldn't buy what they're flogging. Even if they were obliged to tell us the truth about how any growth in our savings will be split between them and us, they'd find some way of avoiding revealing their true costs as most already do. So it's up to us to find out the truth for ourselves. It seems to me that if we were to do simple 'them and us' charts for each financial product we were offered, then we could quickly spot where we're getting value and where we're being taken for complete fools. Though I suspect that a 'them and us' chart, which reveals exactly how much of any growth we get to keep and how much is taken by financial services insiders, is about the last thing any financial products seller would want us to see.

Hopefully *Pillaged* will have started some readers on the journey towards understanding how the financial services industry now works and what we need to do to protect ourselves from its short-termism, greed, avarice and amorality.

References

[1] *Smarter Investing* Tim Hale (FT Prentice Hall 2009).

[2] *www.businesspundit.com* 18 May 2009.

[3] *The Long and The Short of It* John Kay (Erasmus Press 2009).

[4] *Money Mail* 14 October 2009.

[5] *New Statesman* 10 June 2002.

[6] *Huffington Post* 20 March 2009.

[7] *How Markets Fail* John Cassidy (Penguin 2009).

[8] *Huffington Post* 15 April 2010.

[9] *Financial Reform: Five fights to watch* Andy Kroll 14 April 2010.

[10] *The Times* 16 October 2008.

[11] ibid.

[12] TaxPayers' Alliance website, 13 May 2009.

[13] *New York Times* 13 September 2009.

[14] *Why can't we fire failed regulators?* Mark A. Calabria (Cato Institute 9 July 2010).

[15] *Triumph of the regulators* Wall Street Journal 28 June 2010.

[16] Speech at a Financial Services Industry 'summit' meeting, 2003.

[17] *Smarter Investing* Tim Hale (FT Prentice Hall 2006).

[18] *Daily Telegraph* 19 June 2010.

[19] *www.thisismoney.co.uk* 31 March 2010.

[20] *www.marketwatch.com* 10 November 2009.

[21] *Daily Telegraph* 28 September 2010.

[22] Brian Perry – articles on www.investopedia.com.

[23] *The Long and The Short of It* John Kay (Erasmus Press 2009).

[24] *Day Trading Craze Should Give Investors Pause* Philip A. Feigin (NASAA 25 November 1998).

[25] Quotes from responses to an article *Dirty secrets of financial planners*.

[26] *Brilliant Investing* Martin Bamford (Pearson 2008).

[27] *Sunday Times* 15 August 2010.

[28] *Financial Times* 27 August 2010.

[29] *Guardian* 3 May 2008.

[30] *New York Times* 24 July 2009.

[31] *The Intelligent Investor* Benjamin Graham – revised edition with commentary by Jason Zweig (HarperCollins 2003).

[32] ibid.

33 *Daily Telegraph* 29 September 2010.

34 *Challenge to Judgement* Paul Samuelson 1974 and *The Loser's Game* Charles Ellis 1975.

35 *Smarter Investing* Tim Hale (Financial Times/Prentice Hall 2006).

36 *Fundology* John Chatfeild-Roberts (Harriman House 2006).

37 *The 86 Biggest Lies on Wall Street* John R. Talbott (Constable 2009).

38 *Mail on Sunday* 15 September 2008.

39 *Financial Times* 28 March 2007.

40 *The 86 Biggest Lies on Wall Street* John R. Talbott (Constable 2009).

41 *Daily Telegraph* 20 January 2009.

42 *www.thisismoney.co.uk* 27 May 2009.

43 *www.lovemoney.com* 20 January 2009.

44 Spread betting FAQs on *www.financial-spread-betting.com.*

45 ibid.

46 *Daily Telegraph* 5 March 2010.

47 *Independent* 17 May 2007.

48 *CNN* 22 May 2009.

49 *MoneyWeek Asia* 14 September 2010.

50 *Guardian* 14 December 2008.

51 *Guardian* 16 March 2010.

52 *Race to the bottom* Jim Cousins, Austin Mitchell and Prem Sikka (Association for Accountancy & Business Affairs 2004).

53 ibid.

54 Aviva Annual Accounts audited by Ernst & Young LLP.

55 *Banking Crisis: Reforming corporate governance and pay in the City* Treasury Select Committee, September 2008.

56 *Financial advisor seminar marketing* www.financial-seminar.net.

57 *www.thisismoney.co.uk* 14 June 2007.

58 *CBS MarketWatch* 4 April 2003.

59 *How to spot a financial scam* MoneyWeek 9 August 2007.

60 *How to spot an investment scam* www.fool.co.uk April 2009.

61 *Daily Mail* 20 October 2009.

62 *www.thisismoney.co.uk* 5 August 2010.

63 *www.thisismoney.co.uk* 5 August 2010.

64 Pensions Institute, Cass Business School, 16 March 2006.

65 *Financial Times* 16 April 2010.

66 Ibid.

67 One of the better ones I've found is at www.7-secrets.co.uk/SevenSecrets/FIQ/FIQ-Test.htm.

68 *MoneyWeek* 20 August 2010

David Craig worked as a management consultant for almost a hundred organisations in fifteen different countries. After writing *Rip-Off* and *Plundering the Public Sector*, exposing how consultants take millions from their clients while giving little in return, he was blacklisted by the major consultancies. He then turned his attention to examining the incompetence, stupidity, waste, greed and corruption of those who rule us and wrote three books – *Squandered: How Gordon Brown is wasting over one trillion pounds of our money*, *The Great European Rip-Off* and *Fleeced! How we've been betrayed by politicians, bureaucrats and bankers*.

Most recently, when he found out how much of his savings and pension money had been siphoned off by financial services insiders, he wrote *Pillaged* to expose how those working in financial services loot hundreds of millions of pounds a day from our savings and pensions. Thanks to the efforts of some of Britain's best-known financial services firms, David Craig lives in poverty in Bournemouth.